THE SUPERNATURAL IN THE OLD TESTAMENT

THE SUPERNATURAL IN THE OLD TESTAMENT

by

JOHN ROGERSON

*Senior Lecturer in Theology
at the University of Durham*

LUTTERWORTH PRESS

GUILDFORD AND LONDON

First published 1976

Biblical quotations are taken from the Revised Standard Version
(1952), unless otherwise stated

ISBN 0 7188 2233 1

COPYRIGHT © 1976 JOHN ROGERSON

*Text set in 11/12 pt. Photon Imprint, printed by photolithography,
and bound in Great Britain at The Pitman Press, Bath*

CONTENTS

PART I

INTRODUCTION

'In the beginning God created the heavens and the earth' (Genesis 1:1). The Old Testament is a book in which we expect to find statements about God. If Genesis 1 worries us at all, it is not because of its claim that the existence of the world is dependent upon God; our worries are much more likely to be concerned with how we reconcile the biblical claims with scientific views about the origin of the universe. But what about the following passages?

> 'But the serpent said to the woman, "You will not die."' (Genesis 3:4)
> 'And he looked, and lo, the bush was burning, yet it was not consumed.' (Exodus 3:2)
> 'And the Lord went before them by day in a pillar of cloud to lead them along the way, and by night in a pillar of fire to give them light.' (Exodus 13:21)
> 'Now the Spirit of the Lord departed from Saul, and an evil spirit from the Lord tormented him.' (I Samuel 16:14)
> 'The jar of meal was not spent, neither did the cruse of oil fail, according to the word of the Lord which he spoke by Elijah.' (I Kings 17:16)

These texts raise a number of different problems for us. Was there a talking serpent in the Garden of Eden, and before it was cursed to go on its belly, did it somehow maintain an upright posture? How could a bush burn without being consumed? Were the Israelites accompanied through the wilderness by a solid, moving pillar of cloud which turned into fire at night? Does God torment people by sending evil spirits into them? How were the cruse of oil and the jar of meal replenished?

We find these passages, and others like them, difficult, not simply *because* they speak of God or the supernatural, but because of the *way* in which they do it. In some cases, the moral implications of texts also raise difficulties for us, as in the passage about the evil spirit from God which tempted Saul.

It would be a mistake to think that it is only recently that religious people have been bothered by such questions. In fact, thoughtful religious people have been bothered by them for probably well over a thousand years! Rabbi Ada ben Minyomi, who probably lived in the 5th century AD, wondered if Elijah was fed not by ravens, as stated in I Kings 17:6, but by two men who were both named 'Raven'.[1] Saadia ben Joseph (882–942) tried to explain the difficulty that appears in Genesis 18, when Abraham addresses one of his visitors as though that visitor were God (verse 3). Saadia argued that the Bible had used a sort of shorthand expression, and that what was meant was that Abraham recognized the visitor to be an angel.[2] Another great Jewish scholar, Maimonides (1138–1204), maintained that Abraham's meeting with the three men (Genesis 18), Jacob's wrestling with the angel (Genesis 32:22–32), Balaam's talking ass (Numbers 22:22–35) and Gideon's fleece (Judges 6:36–40) had all occurred in visions or dreams to the persons involved.[3]

For at least the last two hundred years, many Christian scholars have tried to help readers to understand difficult supernatural passages by giving to the texts a 'natural' and 'reasonable' explanation. The talking serpent has been explained as an ancient Israelite example of the sort of world-wide folk-tale in which animals speak. The burning bush was perhaps a sunset gleaming through a bush. In the case of the pillar of cloud, perhaps an observer saw a whirlwind in the camp and interpreted it as a sign of God's presence, while the origin of the pillar of fire was in the lighted braziers carried at the head of caravans at night. Saul's evil spirit was the ancient Israelite way of describing what we today would call mental illness or depression, and Elijah's miracles are the sort of story about the deeds of holy men that can be found the world over.

In some cases, such explanations have been guesswork, and nothing more. This is the case with the suggestions about the burning bush and the pillar of cloud. The explanations about the talking serpent and Elijah's miracles are not unsupported guesswork but are based on a comparative study of folklore. What is said about Saul's evil spirit *is* unsupported guesswork, though based on the undoubted fact that the ancient Israelites did not have the psychological concepts and vocabulary that we use today.

Some people are undoubtedly deeply offended by attempts to 'explain away' the supernatural elements in the Old Testament. But many other people are grateful for what has been done. The point has at least been acknowledged in such 'explaining away' that belief in God does not in-

---

[1] Babylonian Talmud, Hullin 5a.

[2] See H. Malter, *Life and Works of Saadia Gaon*, Philadelphia, 1921, pages 107–108.

[3] See *The Guide of the Perplexed*, Part II, Sections 32–48. There are numerous translations of the *Guide*, e.g. by S. Pines, Chicago, 1963.

volve a literalist understanding of the Bible, and that it is permissible to approach the Bible with a questioning, as well as a reverent, attitude of mind.

There is, however, a danger that explanations of the supernatural in 'reasonable' and 'ordinary' terms can go too far. We may throw out the baby with the bath water by making the Old Testament so ordinary and reasonable that we lose sight of all that it says about the mystery and majesty of God. We may come to think of the Old Testament writers not as men of God, with deep spiritual insight, but as naive and prescientific persons who knew no better than to attribute to God what modern science can explain without the need for a God.

It would be foolish for me to claim that I can answer questions and solve problems that have been discussed and written about for a very long time. In the following pages, however, I have tried to give some guidance to teachers, general readers, and perhaps even to clergy, about how we may approach some Old Testament passages which have difficult supernatural elements. The approach is, I hope, both questioning and positive, but aimed at a general readership, and not at my professional Old Testament colleagues. If any of the latter happen to read the book, and find that instead of talking about theophanies and cult traditions I have concentrated on the question 'what really happened?', it is because this last question is the one which usually bothers the general reader most.

The main part of the book is devoted to the exposition of some twenty selected passages from the Old Testament, but it may be helpful if I make clear the principles of my approach.

1. NATURAL AND SUPERNATURAL

Among the definitions of 'supernatural' to be found in the *Oxford English Dictionary* there are the following: 'belonging to a higher realm ... than that of nature' and 'abnormal, extraordinary'. The first definition corresponds roughly to what was written in the first paragraph of the introduction. If we believe in God, we assume that he is not a part of nature, but that he is in some way above it and controlling it; he belongs to a higher realm. Verses such as Genesis 1:1 do not worry us merely because they assert that the world is dependent on a higher 'being', God. We can therefore assume that the general reader is not worried by 'supernatural' in this first sense.

It is with the second sense of 'supernatural' that this book will be largely concerned. We are worried by stories about talking animals, jars of oil that never become empty, and dead persons who are restored to life, because these stories describe what for us is *abnormal* and *extraordinary*. Such stories conflict with our modern belief that the world is essentially orderly, and that this order can be described in terms of 'laws' which abnormal and extraordinary happenings seem to break.

The terms 'natural' and 'supernatural' are not biblical terms, and in their popular use (although not necessarily in their use in traditional theology) they suggest a different understanding of the world from that implied in the Old Testament. Popular use of 'natural' and 'supernatural' implies that nature is a closed system in which God 'intervenes' in events that are abnormal and extraordinary, and it is the extraordinary nature of the events which points to their divine origin. In contrast, passages can be found in the Old Testament which suggest that the Israelites believed that God was responsible for all the *ordinary* processes of nature (see Psalm 104:10–24) and it has been asserted that the Israelites had no concept of miracle in the sense of an abnormal or extraordinary event initiated by God.

However, it may be possible to over-estimate the differences between modern popular thought and Old Testament belief about the world; at all events, the differences must be carefully discussed.

Even if parts of the Old Testament describe God as ordering all the processes of nature, it is still probable that the Israelites recognized order and regularity in nature, and that they carried on their technology on the basis of well-tried rules. Genesis 1:1 ff. implies that at creation, unordered matter was organized into an ordered world, and Genesis 8:22, which promises after the flood that 'while the earth remains, seed time and harvest, cold and heat, summer and winter, day and night, shall not cease' describes observable regularity in nature. The same is true of Psalm 19:1–6, and in Jeremiah 8:7, the prophet contrasts the inconstancy of God's people with the unfailing regularity with which migratory birds journey to and from Judah in due season. In the book of Ecclesiastes, the writer bases some of his apparent scepticism on the regular recurring pattern of events, including events in nature (1:5–7), which he sums up in the observation that there is nothing new under the sun.[4]

Not only can we say that the Israelites recognized order and regularity in nature, but it is clear that they also recognized events that were inconsistent with this regularity and order. They did not expect animals

---

[4] See further the section entitled 'law in the natural process' in W. Eichrodt, *Theology of the Old Testament*, Vol 2, London, 1967, pages 152 ff.

to talk, jars never to be empty, shadows of sundials to go backwards, and dead persons to be restored to life; the whole point about recording the extraordinary achievements of, say, Elijah or Elisha was precisely to emphasize that these men did things that did not happen in the ordinary run of events, and that, therefore, they were special servants of God. In this sense, we could justifiably say that the Israelites did recognize what we would call a miracle (in the sense of something extraordinary or abnormal) even if they had no special word for it.

What we do not know is whether the Israelites had built up a body of abstract theoretical speculation about the order and regularity of the world of nature. Even if they had done so, it is certain that it would have differed from modern theoretical speculation, at least in scope if not more fundamentally. For us today, an eclipse is not an abnormal or extraordinary event; but it was probably just that for ancient Israelites, and if so, to be put in the same category as extraordinary jars of oil and resuscitated corpses. We can conclude that although Israelites, like ourselves, recognized that certain happenings were inconsistent with order and regularity in nature, the Israelite would have included more events in this category than we do. Also, he may have found it easier than we do to believe that such things had actually happened.

Another difference between Old Testament belief and modern popular thought is that the latter is predominantly mechanistic in its view of the world of nature. Whereas we think of the world as a system which works in terms of 'laws', the Israelites probably had a more God-centred view of things, as seen in passages such as Psalm 104:10–24. Regularity and order in nature were perhaps for the Israelites conceived in terms of God's promises (Genesis 8:22) and his faithfulness. The differences between modern popular thought and Old Testament belief can be represented diagrammatically as on page 6.

Several points should be noted. There is no place for 'natural' and 'supernatural' in the Old Testament diagram. Though the latter has a 'miracle' pole, that concept would contain more events than would the 'miracle' pole in the popular thought diagram, for the reasons already explained. Popular thought would recognize fewer miracles, not only because the modern understanding of the regular and ordered is wider than the Old Testament understanding, but also because modern thought will apply the test of historicity to some Old Testament miracles, and will rule them out on these grounds. Thus the word 'historical' appears on the popular thought diagram (page 6), indicating that historicity plays its part in distinguishing between what may be termed miracle, and what may be regarded as deriving from mere superstition or hearsay.

It is now necessary to comment on these two positions from a traditional theological perspective. The 'laws' which in popular thought are supposed to govern the natural order are, in fact, generalizations based on human observation. They do not concern the world 'as it is' (whatever that may be), but the world *as we think about it*. The way we think about it may change in the light of new knowledge, and it could

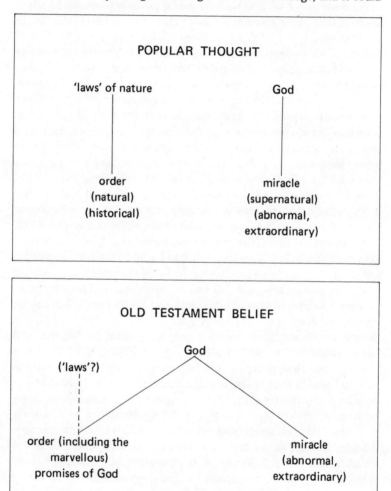

well be that what we today regard as miraculous (that is, abnormal and extraordinary) would be regarded as ordinary by future generations. To describe order in nature in terms of 'laws' does not necessarily exclude God from the world. Indeed, like the Old Testament, the theologian may wish to claim that many regular, ordered things in nature are marvellous, and in some way reflections of God's glory (Psalm 19:1 ff). At the same time, the theologian will be careful about the way he states that God works in and through the ordered things of nature. There are many unpleasant as well as marvellous processes in the natural order ('nature red in tooth and claw') and how God is to be related to these is a concern of theology known as 'theodicy', and cannot be discussed here.[5] The problem of God's relation to the natural order is, again, a problem of *how we think* about God's relation to the world, and it is not inconsistent to affirm our belief that God *is* somehow actively related to the natural order without being able to *say adequately* how this is so. The theological position can also be represented by a diagram, in which the broken lines indicate God's relationship to the world, a relationship which, however, cannot be adequately described.

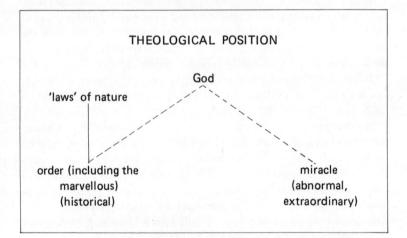

THEOLOGICAL POSITION

God

'laws' of nature

order (including the
marvellous)
(historical)

miracle
(abnormal,
extraordinary)

In this diagram, there is no real place for the natural/supernatural categories that are in the popular thought diagram, for the theologian wishes to assert, with the Old Testament, that some aspects of the ordered world are 'supernatural' in that they express the glory of God or

---

[5] See John Hick, *Evil and the God of Love,* London, 1966.

because God 'works' through them. Miracle is retained, in the sense of the abnormal or extraordinary, though much narrower in scope than for the Old Testament diagram, and the category of history is used to decide whether some alleged miracles are in fact miracles. The Resurrection of Christ is a case where the historical indications are strong (though not, in the nature of the case, conclusive) that Christ rose from death, and this event is thus a miracle in that it is certainly extraordinary and abnormal.

If we compare this diagram with the Old Testament belief diagram, we see that the two have much in common. The Old Testament scope of miracle is wider than that of the modern theologian, and the latter will use both his greater knowledge of order and regularity in nature, as well as his keener historical sense in order to remove from the category of miracle what the Old Testament might have regarded as a miracle.

To which categories will he remove these latter 'miracles'? In some cases, it will be to the category of the marvellous in the ordered world. If the plagues in Egypt were basically natural occurrences, then for the modern writer they were not miracles according to his strict definition. This is not, however, to deny that they were marvellous, for they coincided with Israel's exodus from Egypt and were seen by the Israelites as God's work on their behalf. Thus, to remove the plagues from the category of miracle does not mean that they cease to be regarded as in some sense the work of God. Where the modern writer differs from the Old Testament is merely in the scope of his category of miracle. He is at one with the Old Testament in regarding the plagues as the work of God.

In other cases, the modern writer will remove some Old Testament miracles to a category not represented on the diagrams, that of the non-historical. He may do this for several reasons. He may believe that a miracle story is an unassimilated folk-tale (see section 4). He may conclude that as a story has been passed down from one generation to another by word of mouth, the story has been progressively embellished with extraordinary or abnormal details (see also section 4). He may think that because a story comes from what I call later (in section 6) the third-hand or reported traditions of encounter between God and man, the story has utilized traditional symbols for God's presence, and is therefore not to be taken literally. By calling these traditions non-historical, it is not implied that there is no historical basis to them, but rather that it is impossible with certainty to discover their original historical character. In any case, the importance of these traditions for the theologian will not lie in whether or not they are historically true, but in the way in which they reflect Israel's belief in God. Such points will be emphasized in the expositions of the selected passages.

To conclude this section, throughout the book, the term 'supernatural' is used mainly in its popular sense of abnormal or extraordinary. This is a book for general readers, and the difficulties which the popular usage of 'supernatural' raises for the general reader will be tackled. The difficulties will be tackled, however, in terms of the third diagram, and the explanation which follows and precedes it.

2. MYTH

There is no doubt that the word 'myth' is offensive to some readers, because in its popular sense, it denotes something that did not happen, or which is otherwise untrue. On the whole, the word has been avoided in this book, but my treatment of some of the passages has been affected by the results of my own researches into the concept of myth as used in Old Testament studies.[6] It is, in fact, very difficult to say what myth is, and this is because the word has become a label attached to very many different things. Myths have been defined as stories about gods, as stories which accompanied rituals, as stories which were basically poetic descriptions of the workings of nature; myth has been understood as a particular way of thinking about the world, different from that of modern western man. Because of this variety of definition, I think that it is best to avoid the word myth, and instead to try to identify the problems which the use of the concept of myth (however defined) has tried to solve.

My expositions of selected passages have been influenced by two approaches to myth, which ought to be mentioned here. The first, which affects Genesis 3 in particular (see pages 24ff), has been advanced by the French philosopher Paul Ricoeur.[7] Ricoeur believes that myths are stories which hold together in opposition the apparent contradictory basic symbols which express man's understanding of his existence. In the Old Testament, there are expressed man's convictions that he is a free agent, rightly judged by God when God's will is disobeyed. But there is also an awareness that man is not in complete control of himself; evil is a force outside of himself, stronger than him, and to which he responds from inside of himself. Yet we feel compelled to say both that

---

[6] *Myth in Old Testament Interpretation*, W. de Gruyter, Berlin, 1974.
[7] *Philosophie de la Volonté*, Paris, 1950, II pt. 2, 'La Symbolique du Mal.'

man is fully responsible for the evil that he does, and that he is in some way forced into doing it. This is the paradox of the 'serf-arbitre', the free man who is a slave, and Ricoeur believes that in the story of Genesis 3, these apparent contradictions are held together in story form, not in order to solve the problem that the contradictions raise, for this is impossible, but in order to state at the outset of the Old Testament what the men of God in ancient Israel had learnt of their true being, as they had come to know something about God. How far Ricoeur's understanding of myth will receive any general acceptance remains to be seen, but for the present writer, it sheds a good deal of light on a narrative such as Genesis 3, and shows how the passage can be interpreted in the light of many other parts of the Old Testament.

The second discussion of myth which has influenced the approach to certain narratives in this book is that by Ernst Lohmeyer in the volume *Kerygma and Myth*.[8] This is part of a wider debate about the interpretation of the New Testament which was conducted during and after the second World War. In his essay, Lohmeyer argued,

> how else can we believe in God or speak of the gods, unless we conceive of him or them as working and having their being in this world among us men in the same mode as men speak and work? . . . It is the secret and basis (of all religion) that human conceptions, while they remain human, are nevertheless capable of apprehending the divine and so surpass all human conception.[9]

In this argument, he was trying to maintain that stories about God which describe him as encountering man in this world, in something of the way that a man encounters a man, were stories that did more than merely describe human thoughts about man's existence. Lohmeyer was maintaining that such stories were saying something about the reality beyond this world that we call God, and that it was the inadequacy of human language which necessitated the use of stories in which God was made to speak and work as men speak and work.

In the Old Testament there are a number of stories that could be described in this way, for example, Genesis chapters 18, and 32:22–32. I would want to call them 'myth' in Lohmeyer's sense, and in my expositions, I have tried to express what I think is the reality to which

[8] E. Lohmeyer, 'The Right Interpretation of the Mythological' in H. W. Bartsch (ed.), *Kerygma and Myth*, London, 1964,[2] pages 124 ff.

[9] Lohmeyer, page 126.

they point. However, I would add one further point: although these stories seem to portray God as working and speaking as men do, there is always an element of mystery in their description of the divine. This element of mystery is described further in the section 'Presence and Power' (see page 14).

3. 'ULTIMATE QUESTIONS'

Although there is no discussion later in the book of the incident in I Samuel 16:14 which speaks about the evil spirit from God which tormented Saul, the general problem which it raises is worth discussion. The obvious way of understanding the passage is as follows: the ancient Israelites had no conception of what we call depression or mental illness. Therefore, they ascribed any sort of abnormal human behaviour to God. Thus the story of Saul's evil spirit tells us nothing about God, but something about the difference between our modern understanding of things, and that of the biblical writers.

I think, however, that the matter is more complicated than this, and that when the biblical writer used the concept of the 'evil spirit from God' he was wrestling with what I call an 'ultimate question'. An ultimate question is a question of the type 'why do innocent people suffer?', 'who is ultimately responsible for evil, if not God?'. To such questions, modern philosophical theological thought can give no satisfactory *logical* answer. In the case of Saul, one strand at least of biblical tradition believed that Saul had been appointed on God's initiative (I Samuel 9:1–10:16), and that he had tried to serve his God honestly and zealously (I Samuel 28:3; II Samuel 21:2). The record was also aware of Saul's failures, and it noted his personal reasons for being jealous of David (I Samuel 18:8–9). The main difficulty for the biblical writer, however, was to explain why Saul, who had been chosen by God, had fallen from grace; why his actions had become increasingly desperate, involving murder (I Samuel 22:17–19) and the occult (I Samuel 28:8–9) before his tragic death in battle. Had God made a mistake when he chose Saul? How could the one on whom God's spirit had descended do such deeds?

These problems are similar to those with which the opening of the book of Job and I Kings 22:19–23 wrestle. Both these passages try to deal with ultimate questions, and it is significant that in both passages, something like an evil spirit appears, which has considerable freedom of action, while remaining ultimately responsible to God. I do not believe that the Old Testament, any more than modern theological thought,

11

found the answer to these ultimate questions, but two points are worthy of consideration. Firstly, if we take the story of Saul's evil spirit from God together with Job 1–2 and I Kings 22:19–23, then the Saul story is more than merely a pre-scientific explanation of Saul's moods. It is a much deeper attempt to account for success and failure, obedience and apostasy on the part of a servant of God. Secondly, these Old Testament attempts to solve ultimate questions imply a belief in God that is far from superficial. It would be much easier, especially for ancient and less sophisticated peoples, to solve ultimate questions by believing not in one God, but in two or more opposed cosmic forces, the one (or some) evil, the other (or others) good. Belief in *one* God (and such belief is implicit throughout the Old Testament, even where the existence of other gods is not denied) puts the ultimate questions in their most acute form by creating the problem that a God who is believed to be good and to have created a good world, is ultimately responsible for evil and pain and suffering. The Old Testament writers who were bold enough to assert such a belief had not come to it by philosophical reflection, but through their openness to God, and from the conviction of ancient Israel that God had acted in decisive moments of their history, and in so doing had revealed something of his character. The ancient Israelites and the Old Testament writers may have been pre-scientific in many things, but when we are faced with narratives which appear simply to express a pre-scientific naivety, closer inspection of the text may well reveal that the real problems are philosophical and theological. I do not believe that openness to God is directly related to scientific knowledge.

4. FOLKLORE

The words 'folklore' and 'folk-tale' are likely to upset some readers just as much as the word 'myth'. All peoples seem to have their folk-tales, and it would be surprising if this had not been true for the ancient Israelites.[10] Folk-tales express some of the deepest hopes and longings of the 'ordinary' members of societies. They also often express a concern for the 'under-dog'. So you are likely to find that the stupid youngest son comes out best, or the orphan girl and not her step-mother or step-sisters is the one who marries the prince. Sometimes magical forces come to the aid of the hero or heroine, as they pass through tribulation to success.

---

[10] For a treatment of Old Testament traditions in the light of comparative folklore see T. H. Gaster, *Myth, Legend and Custom in the Old Testament*, London, 1969.

12

Because many of the stories recorded in books such as Genesis, Exodus, Judges and I Samuel were passed down by word of mouth for many generations they must have been influenced by the folk-tales of the ancient Israelites, but we must not necessarily assume that all such influences are bad. On the contrary, such influence probably gave to many stories in the Old Testament their dramatic shape, and helped them to express more clearly the ancient Israelite conviction that God had been active in certain events of their history.

In the section dealing with the Plagues in Egypt (page 38), I have said that I do not believe that in actual fact Moses had a series of interviews with Pharaoh, each of which was followed by a plague which Pharaoh entreated Moses to stop, only for the cycle of Pharaoh's 'obstinacy-plague-entreaty' to happen all over again. Probably, the Israelites escaped from Egypt at a time of great confusion in that country, a confusion which included a number of natural catastrophes. It was in the telling and re-telling of the story of the great deliverance that the whole complex of happenings began to assume the dramatic story form that it now has in Exodus 6–9. Moreover, because in folk-tales it is the under-dog who wins through, often assisted by magical forces, the contact between folk-tales and the telling of the story of the plagues enabled the latter better to express the underlying conviction of the Israelites that their deliverance from Egypt was an act of mercy on the part of God towards a people in need (under-dogs), accompanied by evidence of his power over nature.

There are probably four ways, at least, in which folk-tale or tales have played a part in the formation of some Old Testament passages.

(*a*) A passage may contain elements taken from folk-tale (for example, the talking serpent in Genesis 3).

(*b*) The influence of folk-tale may have shaped the story of an historical occurrence, and helped to express Israel's belief in God's action in it (for example, the traditions about the plagues in Egypt).

(*c*) A pure folk-tale may have been deeply assimilated into the Old Testament tradition so as to express something of the distinctive theology of the Old Testament (for example, Genesis 32:22–32 (the story of Jacob's wrestling at the river Jabbok) where several such folk-tales have probably been assimilated).

(*d*) A folk-tale may have entered the biblical tradition with little or no assimilation to the distinctive faith of ancient Israel (for example, the story of Gideon's fleece, Judges 6:36–46)

Of these four ways, only the last is probably of little value to modern readers of the Old Testament.

5. 'PRESENCE' AND 'POWER'

There seem to be some typical differences between narratives that deal with God's *presence* and those that deal with his *power*.

(*a*) Examples of the *presence* of God narratives are the visit of the three men to Abraham (Genesis 18), the call of Moses (Exodus 3 : 1–12) and Jacob's wrestling (Genesis 32 : 22 ff). A typical feature of such stories is a certain confusion between God and his messengers. Thus in Genesis 18, the three men appear to symbolize the presence of God, one of them is addressed as though he *were* God, yet God seems to speak directly to Abraham from heaven. In the incident of Jacob's wrestling, it is far from clear whether Jacob is wrestling with a man, an angel, with God, or with all of them at once! In the story of the burning bush, there is an apparent confusion between the angel who appears to Moses 'in a flame of fire out of the midst of the bush' (Exodus 3 : 2) and God who calls to Moses 'out of the bush'. Some of these apparent confusions may be due to the fact that the stories as they now stand are composed of several originally separate strands of tradition; but as I later note (page 35) not all of the apparent confusions can be removed by supposing that they result from the combination of different sources. While I do not claim to be able to explain satisfactorily why the apparent confusions are there if they did not result from the combination of separate sources, I believe that their presence in the narratives is not an accident.

Narratives about God's *presence* seem to be confined to traditions about what happened in Israel before Israel had a king. They are all third-hand not first-hand traditions (I shall explain the importance of this distinction shortly). It is likely that when the biblical writers came to describe the encounters with God that had taken place in the earliest times of Israelite history, they believed that God had revealed himself more directly to these men of old, compared with the way he was believed to reveal himself at the time of the biblical writers. Thus in the narratives about the encounters with God experienced by figures such as Abraham, Jacob and Moses, the biblical writers portrayed the encounters as vivid and direct meetings with the divine; yet the presence of apparent confusions in the narratives between God and his messengers helped to preserve a sense of mystery about the incidents.

(*b*) Narratives about the *power* of God are much more widely distributed throughout the Old Testament, and they constitute the bulk of what we normally regard as miracle stories. In these stories about God's power, many folk-tale elements appear which have not been assimilated into the tradition so as to express any part of the distinctive faith of the Old Testament (compare the miracles of Elisha in II Kings 4: 38–44). In many of these stories, the *historical* problem of 'what really happened' is at its most acute, and although each case must be judged on its merits, it is in the area of these stories about God's power that the reader will most frequently find himself in conflict with the Old Testament text. Taken as a whole, these stories about God's power express the conviction that God is in control of the world and the happenings in it. But these stories have to be set beside the many other Old Testament passages which assert that God is working through many ordinary and non-spectacular happenings. (See section 1, *Natural and Supernatural.*)

6. THIRD-HAND AND FIRST-HAND TRADITION

Many people who read Old Testament narratives about the presence and power of God are bothered by the fact that in their day-to-day religious experience, they know of nothing comparable to what is recorded in the Old Testament. We do not see burning bushes or hear God's voice speaking audibly to us, though we may allow that very exceptionally people genuinely claim to have had such experiences. However, the Old Testament contains much that *does* match the experience of ordinary people. The Psalms, for instance, fully express the range of religious experiences familiar to modern man. God is sometimes close to the psalmist, and sometimes seems to be far off. The psalmist is filled now with faith, and now with doubt. One moment he can utter sublime praises to God, and in the next breath he can express his hatred for his enemies.

The prophetic books, too, record much about experience of God that the ordinary religious man can appreciate and they sometimes show us the ordinary 'mechanics' of how the divine message came to the prophets. The similarity of the Hebrew words for 'summer fruits' and 'end' triggered off for Amos a message about divine judgement when he saw a basket of summer fruits (Amos 8: 1–3). Jeremiah received a message whilst watching a potter at work (Jeremiah 18: 1–11).

These passages from the Psalms and the prophetic books represent what I have called the first-hand accounts of divine-human encounter. They are not necessarily autobiographical, but they are probably dependent on and reflect a personal tradition of encounter with God. In many

15

cases they stress the ordinariness and the indirectness of the encounter. In contrast, I describe as third-hand, or belonging to the reported tradition about encounter with God, those traditions which come especially in books such as Genesis, Exodus, Numbers and Joshua. Here, a kind of shorthand is used to describe the encounter with God, precisely because people like Moses were too far removed in time from the writers of the Old Testament for a first-hand tradition to go back to them. We shall never know the exact nature of the experience of God in the life of Moses. This means that especially in the opening books of the Old Testament, phrases such as 'The Lord said unto Moses' are not to be taken literally, as though Moses actually heard a voice. We can assume that this is shorthand, expressing the Old Testament conviction that Moses did in some way receive divine communications, though it would be reasonable to suppose that in fact his experience was not essentially different from that described in what I call the first-hand tradition.

It is to be acknowledged that this distinction is a rough and ready one, and that it leaves much unsaid. For example, in Amos 7:8 we have the phrase 'The Lord said unto me', and it is well known that narratives such as the call of Moses (Exodus 3) were influenced by the pattern assumed by first-hand accounts of calls to prophets (for example, by Isaiah 6 and Jeremiah 1). Moreover, even a first-hand account of religious experience tends to be expressed in certain typical or traditional phrases (compare testimonies of religious conversion), and this is true of the first-hand tradition in the Old Testament. Whatever the inadequacies of my first-hand/third-hand or reported distinction, I believe that it will help the reader to understand some of the Old Testament narratives where encounter with God is described in terms quite outside his ordinary experience, and I believe that the distinction can be to some extent tested out in one of the practical activities for individual or group use, at the end of the book.

7. SOURCES AND TRADITIONS

Old Testament scholars have believed for many generations that some books of the Old Testament, especially books like Genesis and Exodus, reached their present form when an editor or editors wove together what were originally separate written sources. The earliest *observations* along these lines go back at least 1,000 years! The reader who has not met this view before is recommended to read Genesis 6:5–9:17 in the Authorised, Revised or Revised Standard Version, or the New English Bible. It is easy to discern large blocks of material in

16

which either the name 'God' appears, or in which the divine name is 'the Lord' (6:5–8, 7:1–5, 8:6–12, though there is no divine name in the last reference, 8:20–22 for 'the Lord' passages; 6:9–22, 7:7–23 although 'the Lord' occurs in verse 16, 8:1–5, 13–19, 9:1–17, for 'God' passages). These blocks of material represent two originally separate written accounts of the Flood.

In my explanations of passages, I have insisted strongly that it is the narrative *as it now stands* which must be interpreted, and not what scholars suggest about a narrative's possible earlier stages. However, I have often referred to sources and traditions that possibly underlie the narratives, in order to help the reader to see why there is unevenness in some passages, and why some elements seem not to fit the main theme of the story. Where I speak of the Yahwist source, I refer to a collection of traditions written down probably in the 10th or 9th century BC. Where I speak of the Priestly source, I mean a collection of traditions probably written down in the 6th or 5th century BC. The dates suggested for the time of writing down of the sources do not imply that everything to be found in a source had no existence in any form before the written compilation was made; nor do I exclude the possibility that when the written compilations were made, they incorporated *already-written* material. By traditions, as opposed to sources, I mean the smaller units which were gathered together into the two main written sources.

8. MIRACLES AND HISTORICITY

The philosophical and definition problems of miracles have been mentioned in the first section of this introduction (pages 3ff). Here, I propose to outline the question at the historical level: how do we decide which miracles happened?

Where we have a group of miracle stories, as in the Elijah/Elisha cycles, in which the miracles performed can be paralleled from miracles related in other folk literatures, it is likely that those similar Old Testament miracles attributed to Elijah and Elisha did not happen. We have already noted that in the Elijah/Elisha cycles, we have our largest body of unassimilated folk-tales in the Old Testament (see page 15), and as in other folk literatures, the miraculous element in the stories has been produced by the exaggerations that occur as the stories are told and re-told. However, I do not believe that every miracle in the Elijah/Elisha cycles is to be explained in this way. Some of the miracle stories in this part of the Old Testament are self-contained, or merely tacked on to the end of another narrative, while other miracle stories are vital to a quite complicated piece of narrative. The extent to which a narrative is embedded in its context is an important factor when we come to try to interpret it. Thus, there is a lot of difference between many of the Elijah/Elisha stories and the incidents of the drought and the fire from heaven (I Kings 17–18). These last two incidents are closely connected together, and they do not just involve groups of the disciples of the prophets, but concern the Israelite king and nation. Thus, in my exposition of this passage, I shall treat it differently from many of the other miracle stories.

Another way in which miracle stories have come into being in the Old Testament is by the operation of the third-hand process. As writers tried to describe how God disclosed himself to his people in the ancient times of Abraham, Jacob and Moses, they heightened the wonder element precisely because they used their third-hand shorthand language about the encounter, and its mystery.

Miracle stories, then, must be assessed according to their literary type and aim, and their relation to the context in which they occur. The clues provided by such assessments will help us in our historical exercise of trying to reconstruct 'what really happened'.

Ultimately, I would want to go most of the way with the view of miracles and the supernatural in the Old Testament, expressed by one of the greatest Old Testament scholars of our generation, the late Professor H. H. Rowley:

> If miracle be defined as divine activity within the world, a belief in its possibility would seem to be fundamental to a belief in God. He cannot be excluded from the world he has made, or reduced to the position of a spectator of the interplay of forces which he had once set in motion. In the faith of Israel he was too real and personal to be reduced to impotence in his own world, or regarded as one who idly watched while men worked out their own destiny, and this faith is integral to any worth-while faith in God. Many of the miracles recorded in the Old Testament are examples of divine activity through natural events, such as the deliverance from Egypt through wind and wave, from Sisera through storm, or from Sennacherib through plague. Others are examples of divine activity through events which were contrary to the order of nature, such as the passage through walls of water at the Red Sea, the standing still of the sun in the time of Joshua, the recovery of an axe head by Elisha by the device of throwing wood into the water, or the delivery of the three youths from Nebuchadnezzar's fire. In some cases these stories are dramatic representations of simpler facts, as may be seen by a study of the context in which

18

they are set; or wonder tales that grew round the name of a hero; or parabolic stories that were made the vehicle of a message. The miracle stories can neither be uncritically accepted as historical, nor uncritically rejected as fancy. Each example must be examined for itself, in the light of the character of the narrative in which it stands and the purpose for which it appears to have been written. But that there is a truly miraculous element in the story I am fully persuaded. We have not merely the working out of human impulses and the chance interplay of natural forces. We have the activity of God in inspiration and revelation, and the evidence of his presence in Nature and history.[1]

---

[1] H. H. Rowley, *The Faith of Israel*, SCM, London, 1956, pages 58–59.

PART II

SELECT PASSAGES

1

THE CREATION

Genesis 1:1–2:4a

Two major difficulties are probably felt by modern readers of the first chapter of the Bible. The first is how to reconcile the biblical account of creation with scientific theories; the second arises because many commentaries compare Genesis 1 with creation stories from Israel's neighbours in the ancient Near East.

Although the majority of professional theologians and biblical scholars have long since ceased to be bothered by the reconciling of Genesis 1 with scientific theories, the same is not true foɪ many ordinary readers. 'God versus science' still arouses great interest. In 1972, the BBC Radio Four service devoted some two hours to an evening programme on the subject, and from time to time, new scientific theories such as the 'big bang' theory of creation arouse interest among those who look for scientific confirmation of the Bible.

In dealing with the problem, it will be difficult to do other than repeat well-known arguments. First, scientific method is concerned, among other things, with generalization and attempted explanation. It observes phenomena, and tries to make generalizations or hypotheses about them. In the nature of the case, such explanations or hypotheses cannot be *proved*, they can only be *falsified* or be found to be *inadequate*. When this happens, new hypotheses are framed, and these form the basis of scientific explanation until such time as *they* are found to be inadequate in the light of new knowledge or experimentation. Thus there is no finality, especially in such a matter as the origin of the universe. Science involves a continuous discovery of facts, and a continuous framing of hypotheses to account for them.

Genesis 1 undoubtedly contains an element of Hebrew science. Not only has it long been known that in the picture of the world implied in the opening verses—a flat earth enclosed by a semi-spherical dome (the firmament) above which were waters (the waters above the firmament) etc—the Hebrews shared a scientific outlook with other peoples of the ancient Near East, but recent suggestions by anthropologists have shed more light on the scientific outlook underlying the account. It has been suggested that Genesis 1, with its distinctions between light and darkness, water and earth, above the firmament and below the firmament, and so on, displays the sort of classification in terms of opposites that characterizes the perception of the world by 'primitive' peoples as well as modern scientific classification. According to this suggestion, man, however primitive or sophisticated, can only order the mass of sense impressions that come in upon him by dividing them, in terms of opposites, into larger and smaller classes of things that have certain features in common. Thus in Genesis 1, the earth is distinguished from the seas, and the earth-creatures from the sea-creatures; but within earth, trees and plants which are self-propagating are distinguished from the animals which must mate in order to reproduce. This suggestion, then, tells us a lot about why many of the details in Genesis 1 are presented in the way that they are.

If Genesis 1 *contains* 'science', it follows that this science can be no more final than any other science. Just as the scientific explanations of the 1970's have superseded those of the 1870's, and will in turn themselves be superseded by those of the 2070's, so those of Genesis 1 will never now be anything more than evidence for what people thought about the scientific nature of the world nearly 3000 years ago. But this is not to say that Genesis 1 is therefore devoid of all value. It is often said that science can only deal with the 'how' of things and not the 'why'—which is a popular way of saying that theological statements (and most of Genesis 1 is theology) are different from scientific statements. Thus it has been repeatedly asserted that the science of Genesis 1 is not important. What matters is what the narrative has to say about God's relation to the world.

At this point, however, we meet the second difficulty mentioned at the outset of this section. For almost as long as commentators have asserted that the theology implied in Genesis 1 is not in conflict with scientific theories, they have also asserted that Genesis 1 is a Hebrew version of a story about the creation of the world that was well known in the ancient Near East. The basis of this theory was the discovery, in the 1870's, of the Babylonian account of creation (although some features of this Babylonian account had been known, for example, from 4th century AD reports of Eusebius of Caesarea). Although it has been illuminating to read expositions of Genesis 1 in the light of other accounts of creation from the ancient Near East, it is also arguable that such expositions have done less justice to wider theological questions because attention has been focused on how the belief of ancient Israel differed from that of her neighbours. The ordinary reader has been given treatments of Genesis 1 which described the *distinctive features* of the Hebrew as against the other accounts of creation, but he has not necessarily been told how Genesis 1 can teach him something about God in spite of its antiquated science.

All new discoveries tend to influence scholarly theory more than the evidence warrants, and later generations of scholars then correct the balance. In the case of Genesis 1, there appears to be a growing tide of opinion against regarding it merely as a Hebrew version of an ancient popular creation story. If many scholars do not go so far as to make such a denial, they are at least ready to allow that Genesis 1 should be interpreted more in terms of its own structure and ideas than in contrast to its ancient Near Eastern background. The case for the denial of a connexion between Genesis 1 and the Babylonian story is briefly as follows. The Babylonian version consists of two main elements—first, the story of a battle between the gods, and second, the creation of the world by the victorious god, Marduk. Clearly, Genesis 1 has nothing corresponding to the first main element, and it is not absolutely clear that the parallels between Genesis 1 and the second element demonstrate a connexion. (The cases are clearly set out and discussed in A. Heidel, *The Babylonian Genesis,* Chicago, 1951.) However, it has been argued that *traces* of the first element, that a battle between the gods, can be found in Old Testament passages such as Psalm 89:10 and Isaiah 51:9–10 where God's defeat of powers of chaos are mentioned, thus proving that both elements of the Babylonian story were known to the ancient Hebrews, although the first element was not *directly* used in Genesis 1, apart from possible echoes of it in Genesis 1:2.

Against this, it has been maintained that the Babylonian story is untypical of the literature of the period in combining the two elements. There are creation stories from the ancient Near East which contain no account of a battle between gods, while there are accounts of battles between gods which do not lead on to creation. Thus there is no firm evidence that Genesis 1 is connected with any story in which the creation is preceded by a battle between gods. Further, the chapter itself shows signs of the combination of several different, and perhaps originally separate, elements.

First, and best known, is the six-day scheme into which the creative acts have been placed. But there are not six, but eight creative acts, necessitating that two acts of creation take place on the third and sixth days. Moreover, there are ten instances of the phrase 'God said' (verses 3, 6, 9, 11, 14, 20, 24, 26, 28, 29). It has also been noticed that in addition to the verb 'created', the verb 'made' is found in the chapter (for example, verses 7, 16, 25) and an original strand characterized by this latter verb has been surmised. It looks, then, as though it is too simple to regard Genesis 1 as a Hebraized version of the Babylonian story. Whatever the connexions, if any, the chapter gives indications of its own long process of composition, in which the end product has not obliterated traces of various originally separate strands or ideas.

This makes us look to the chapter itself for clues to its theological significance. Two words in particular have received attention. The verb translated 'created' (Hebrew: *bara*) is used in the Old Testament only of God's creative activity, and although some commentators have made too much of this fact, it can safely be concluded that the use of *bara* indicates that the creative process, where God is concerned, is unlike any other creative process. Already, then, the biblical text is stating in its own way what modern theology would say differently, that statements about God's activity are not the same sort of statements as those concerning processes within the natural universe.

If *bara* has important theological connotations, it is the more so true of the verb 'said' in the phrases 'God said'. The model of creation by means of the spoken word (which is not in itself unique to the ancient Israelites) not only asserts a relation between the Creator and creation, but leaves the exact nature of the relation sufficiently unspecified to allow the transcendence of God to be maintained. The notion of the 'word of God' in the whole of the Old Testament has also to be taken into account. According to the Old Testament, God discloses his will to his servants the prophets by means of his word, and the great crises of ancient Israel's history have been foreknown and faced through prophetic reception and proclamation of the word. God has revealed his will to his people in the ten words (Deuteronomy 4:13 see RV margin) or commandments of Mount Sinai, which detail a man's duties to God and his neighbour.

Genesis 1 is thus asserting the dependence of the created order on the God who has made himself known to Israel through the prophetic interpretation of significant events in the life of the people. Because this God is a God who speaks his word to his people through prophet and priest, and who calls Israel to loyalty to himself as a person, the God whose word brings the created order into being is no abstraction or first cause, but one who makes moral and personal demands, in obedience to which alone the true nature of the Creator and the creation can be understood.

These, then, are the lines along which the teaching of Genesis 1 is to be sought. Not as opposed to modern science, nor in distinction to other ancient Near Eastern texts is it best understood, but in terms of its own structures and key words, and against the general background of Old Testament belief. Genesis 1 stands or falls with the rest of the Old Testament and cannot be isolated from it.

Several points of translation and interpretation call for comment:

Does Genesis 1 imply *creatio ex nihilo* (creation out of nothing)? Since the fourth Lateran Council of 1215, *creatio ex nihilo* has been an article of the Christian faith, although it is not explicitly mentioned in the Apostles' and Nicene creeds. If the doctrine is supposed to mean that God did not create the world out of any pre-existent matter, it has to be said that this problem probably did not occur to the Hebrews in this way. If, however, the doctrine asserts the uniqueness of God, and the *dependence* of the created order in some sense on him, then this can be supported from Genesis 1.

An allied question concerns the translation of Genesis 1 : 1. It has long been argued that this should be translated 'When God began to create the heavens and the earth (now the earth was waste and void . . . upon the face of the waters) God said: Let there be light', although the New English Bible is the first 'authorized' version to put something like this down as the main text. Such renderings have often been justified by referring to the Babylonian account, where the world is created from the carcass of the defeated goddess Tiamat, of whom an echo has often been detected in the Hebrew word translated 'waste' (verse 2). Also, there has sometimes been an over-reaction against the more traditional rendering because of the way in which it has been made to support the doctrine of *creatio ex nihilo*.

Although the traditional translation is not free from difficulty, I do not believe that Genesis 1 began with such a complicated sentence as the New English Bible rendering implies. The opening 'In the beginning God created the heaven and the earth' is probably a summary of all that follows. The passage then goes on to describe the formless matter out of which an ordered universe was created. The question whether God also created the formless matter, or how it had otherwise got there, probably did not bother the Hebrew writers. The New English Bible translates the phrase 'spirit of God' of verse 2 as 'a mighty wind'. Again, although this translation is theoretically possible, I do not think that this is what the Hebrew phrase conveyed to the ancient Israelites. If the traditional translation is correct, the passage indicates that divine influence was not absent from the formless matter which was to be the basis of the creation. The whole creation is thus from the beginning 'good' (verse 4 etc) and we are reminded that the account is more concerned with the moral character of the creation dependent upon a holy God, than with speculation about the origin of matter out of which the universe may or may not have been formed.

It goes without saying that scientific theory makes no attempt to comment on the moral character of the universe. To detached observation, the universe is both good and bad, both wonderful and barbaric. Only in commitment to the God who speaks through his word in its various forms, can one have faith in the moral character and purpose of the creation, and Genesis 1 takes this commitment for granted.

2

THE FALL

Genesis 2:4b–3:24

The story of the Garden of Eden and the 'fall' has, like Genesis 1, been compared with traditions from outside the Bible; but it, too, shows signs of being composed of several originally separate strands of tradition, and it must be interpreted in terms of its own final structure. Probably the closest parallel to our passage from outside the Bible is the incident in the *Epic of Gilgamesh*[1] where a serpent deprives Gilgamesh of the plant which bestows immortality. In the *Myth of Adapa*[2], the hero on good advice, refuses bread and water, only to be told that he has lost immortality by his refusal. On a famous Babylonian seal[3] (which is a

---

[1] The *Epic of Gilgamesh* is a text that was widely known in the ancient Near East, parts of which date from at least 1500 BC. The *Epic* is known to us mainly from texts found in the library of Ashurbanipal (669–627) at Nineveh. For translations of the Epic see A. Heidel, *The Gilgamesh Epic and Old Testament Parallels*, Chicago, 1949 and J. B. Pritchard (ed.), *Ancient Near Eastern Texts*, Princeton, 1955, pages 237 ff.

[2] *The Myth of Adapa* was also widely known in the ancient Near East, and fragments of the text were found at El Amarna (Egypt—14th century BC) and the library of Ashurbanipal. See *Ancient Near Eastern Texts*, pages 101 ff.

[3] The seal is reproduced, for example, in J. B. Pritchard (ed.), *Ancient Near East in Pictures*, Princeton, 1969.

hazardous parallel since it has no accompanying text) is portrayed a tree with fruit upon it, two clothed figures, male and female, sitting upon stools, with hands outstretched towards the fruit, and a serpent erect upon its tail.

In the biblical story, the following separate themes can be discerned:

(a) there is a pun on the Hebrew words for Adam and earth (Adam—Hebrew 'ādām, earth—Hebrew 'adāmāh, Genesis 2:7, 3:19). This suggests that there was originally a separate story explaining why, among the ancient Hebrews, man had to till the ground in order to live, and why he was buried in the ground when he died.

(b) the story of the creation of woman, with more Hebrew word-play ('īsh (=man)—'ishshāh (=out of man), compare 2:23) and a link with the verse (2:24) which explains the marriage institution.

(c) various other explanations: why serpents go on their bellies (3:14), why humans wear clothes (3:7, 21), why husbandry is hard work (3:17–19) and why childbirth is painful (3:16).

(d) many commentators hold that the material about the tree of life was originally a separate unit because apart from its mention in 2:9 and 3:22–24, it plays no part in the story.

It is not the place here to discuss in what manner these possible originally separate elements were woven together to give us the story as we now have it. Although many commentaries and monographs have attempted to do this, no large measure of agreement has been reached, and, in any case, attempts to interpret hypothetical original forms of the story divert attention away from the text as it stands.

The general reader will probably be less interested in the literary history of Genesis 2–3, and more concerned with the following questions: were Adam and Eve historical persons? did the Hebrews believe that the serpent actually spoke? how did the eating of the fruit affect Adam and Eve—was it the act of disobedience in eating the fruit or something about the fruit itself which 'opened their eyes'?

A few Christians may feel that they must believe that Adam and Eve were real persons because St Paul apparently believed so, and based his doctrine of sin, death, redemption, and the contrast between Adam and Christ on this belief (Romans 5:12–17). But should New Testament opinions about the Old Testament determine the interpretation of the Old Testament? Most Old Testament scholars would say no; and most New Testament scholars would say that we can accept what St. Paul is saying here, without accepting his views on Adam and Eve. In Romans

5:12–17, St Paul was trying essentially to say two things: first, that although sin was not reckoned until the law was given by Moses, sin and death were nevertheless present in the world *before* the giving of the law; second, that as Adam symbolizes a humanity that is characterized by sin and death, Christ sets men free from both. St Paul's first point was a problem of concern to 1st century Jews, and could only be conducted by means of the sort of arguments likely to be convincing to Jews at that time. It is not a problem likely to worry readers of this book. St Paul's second point will surely be accepted by Christians whatever their views about Adam and Eve.

What makes it impossible for most modern readers to accept the historicity of Adam and Eve is the fact that we know that earliest man was a hunter and food gatherer rather than the settled agriculturalist that Adam was, according to Genesis 2–3. Also, although monogenism (the theory that the human race originated from one group or pair of humans in one part of the world) cannot be entirely discarded, experts tend more towards the view that the human race 'emerged' from more than one centre of the world.[4] Had St Paul lived at a time when he knew these facts, he would no doubt have conducted his argument differently, but it is certain that his basic assertions would have been unaltered. He would have proclaimed that all mankind is subject to sin and death, and that Christ sets men free from both. The same is true of the doctrine of 'original sin'. What is important about the doctrine is not *how* a tendency to do evil is transmitted from generation to generation, but *that* each generation is prone to sin. It has to be noted further, however, and this is of great importance, that to say that mankind is prone to sin is not to make an assertion merely based on general observation. 'Sin' is a *theological* word, and we can only truly learn what sin is by drawing closer to God. Sin itself can dull our awareness of it. The writer, or final editor of Genesis 2–3, had this in common with St Paul and the framers of the doctrine of original sin, that his description of the human condition derived from his experience of closeness to God and not only from general observation. It expressed his understanding of himself in the light of his closeness to God and it summed up a similar awareness within the Israelite community.

The answer to the question whether the ancient Israelites believed that the serpent actually spoke is usually 'yes'. It is often said that the Israelites, like primitive peoples, would have no difficulty in believing in

---

[4] A popular treatment of this particular problem is to be found in the UNESCO magazine *Courier*, August–September 1972.

a beginning time when animals spoke. The same question arises with regard to Balaam's ass (Numbers 22:21–35), Jotham's fable (Judges 9:7–15) and the fable of Jehoash (II Kings 14:9–10). In the case of the two fables, the Israelites were probably well able to appreciate that trees and plants do not normally speak, and that the fables were stories, and not meant as serious history. I think that we should also allow that many, if not most Israelites did not take the speaking animals of Genesis 3 and Numbers 22 as serious history either, and that they regarded the point of the stories as lying elsewhere than in their historicity.

For the origin of the talking serpent and the forbidden fruit we must probably look, as has long been recognized, to folk-tales. Many stories about serpents and magic fruits are found in folk-tales the world over, and it is in folklore that animals speak.

It is also folklore which provides the answer to the question whether the fruit itself or the act of disobedience 'opened the eyes' of Adam and Eve. It was probably the magical effects of the fruit itself which 'opened their eyes', although of course the fruit could not have been eaten without the act of disobedience. Granted that the writer or final editor combined folk-tale elements about a serpent and a forbidden fruit with the other elements mentioned earlier, what does the whole story mean? In its present form it has, from start to finish, a dramatic structure which makes it a whole. Although the tree of life may have come from an originally separate unit, it is necessary for the conclusion of the story—the driving of Adam and Eve from Eden (3:22–24). Again, although many scholars argue that 3:14–19 was originally a separate unit, 3:19 makes sense only in the light of 2:7 and 3:23.

I have already outlined my understanding of Genesis 3 in the Introduction (page 9). It explains many features of ordinary life—marriage, childbirth, work—but it also says something about the human condition as understood through ancient Israel's encounter with God. Through that encounter, Israel had learned that God was just, merciful and holy. Man was unfaithful to God and unjust to his neighbour, and God's judgements were consequently deserved. Yet evil, while not residing in God, was a force both outside of man, and within him. Although in one sense man was free and therefore responsible for his wrongdoings, in other ways he was a prisoner in the power of evil, while still recognizing the justice of God's judgements against human wrongdoing.

In Genesis 2–3, these apparent contradictions are not given a philosophical solution, for such a solution is impossible; rather, they are brought and held together. The serpent is described as one of the creatures which God made (Genesis 3:1), so that there is no suggestion that there is a power of evil which from the beginning was independent of God. Yet at the same time, the serpent does symbolize a power of evil outside of man—a power of evil which seeks to be allied with man's inner desires for self-advancement. In 3:6 the psychology of temptation is described in masterly fashion:

> when the woman saw that the tree was good for food, and that it was a delight to the eyes, and that the tree was to be desired to make one wise, she took of its fuit and ate.

3:8 expresses the sense of alienation from God which sin entails, while in 3:10–13 Adam and Eve try to avoid responsibility for their disobedience.

It is often said that apart from a possible connexion with Ezekiel 28:11 ff., Genesis 3 is never referred to in the rest of the Old Testament, and the conclusion is thus often drawn that the ancient Israelites did not know, or paid little heed to, the teaching that modern interpreters believe it to possess. However, it is unlikely that a story which came to be put in such a significant position in the Old Testament can have had no importance in ancient Israel. Indeed, much that we find in the Psalms and the prophets about the human condition expresses the same apparent contradictions that are held together in Genesis 3; for example, Psalm 51:3–5, and the prophetic description of sinful Israel as a faithless wife.

Genesis 3 expresses a view of the human condition which is not primarily based on general observation of human behaviour, but which springs from the insights afforded by the closeness to God of the men of the Old Testament. That is why no adequate theology can avoid coming to grips with this passage.

3

ABRAHAM'S THREE VISITORS

Genesis 18

Genesis 18 is a narrative about the *presence* of God. It is characterized by a 'confusion' between the three men who visit Abraham, and God who speaks to Abraham directly. It is tempting to explain the difficulties by assuming that our present narrative is composed of several originally separate units, in one of which God spoke directly to Abraham, in another of which a divine messenger dealt with Abraham, and in a third of which Abraham welcomed three guests. But on the whole, critics have not tried to solve the difficulties in this way.

One recent commentator has described the relation between the three men and God as 'problematical'. 18:1 begins by saying that God appeared to Abraham by the oaks of Mamre. In verse 2, on lifting up his eyes, Abraham saw three men, and although he recognized them as important, he did not regard any one of them as divine. In verse 3 (see the detailed discussion later) Abraham addresses a singular 'my lord', presumably directing his speech to the leader of the group. In verses 5 and 9, the three men speak, but in verse 10 we return abruptly to the singular. In verse 13 God explicitly speaks, but in verse 16 the men leave Abraham on their way to Sodom, after which God enters into dialogue with Abraham. Verse 21 makes God say 'I will go down and see . . .' as though he has been absent from the scene hitherto, a point clearly contradicted earlier, for example in verse 10.

Some interpretations have tried to smooth out the difficulty in verse 3, where Abraham addresses a 'my lord' by altering the Hebrew vowels so as to read 'my lords' (so NEB '"Sirs" he said, "if I have deserved your favour . . ."'). This is quite possible, but does not remove the other difficulties.

The relation between the three men and God has been explained in two main ways. First, that one of them was God, the one who spoke in verse 10, and the other two were the angels who went on to Sodom and Gomorrah in Chapter 19. The second is that God was somehow present in all three men (this interpretation does not commit us to seeing a prefiguring of the Trinity although many early Christian commentators did argue this). The second suggestion is more likely to be correct, as it is doubtful whether the writer would have wanted to be so crude as to suggest that God himself visited Abraham in the guise of a traveller.

The exact relation between the travellers and God is, however, less important than the fact that whether deliberately or not, the confusion in the narrative expresses the transcendence and immanence of God. The three men symbolize the presence of God, but only obscurely. God remains in heaven yet he is active in the affairs of men, and concerned with matters such as the disappointments of an elderly childless couple. He speaks his word of promise, and his message is received, even if it is hard to believe. This narrative tries to draw aside a veil to permit us to see something of the mystery of what is for many a daily miracle—that of hearing and obeying God's word.

4

THE SACRIFICE OF ISAAC
Genesis 22:1–19

The questions about this passage which have worried both general readers and commentators have been moral questions. Does God put people to the test in the way that Abraham was tested? Would God command a person to sacrifice his own son? On the whole, commentators have answered both these questions by 'no', and have then tried to explain why it is that the Old Testament itself implies the answer 'yes' to both questions! A common argument has been that a story such as the offering of Isaac could only have arisen and been accepted among a people where the rights of the individual were not fully recognized, and where child sacrifice was practised or known to be practised. It has been maintained that the story marks the point in ancient Israel's history when it was realized that God did not want human sacrifice. Another view has interpreted the story as a cult legend preserved at a sanctuary, and explaining why animal offerings had been substituted for child offerings.

It is not the intention of the comments that follow to deny the impressive evidence set out in the commentaries that human sacrifice was practised in the ancient Near East, and even in ancient Israel. It is also possible either that the story marks a general protest in Israel against child sacrifice, or that it originated in a similar sense at a particular cult centre. The main question is from what angle should the story as it now stands be approached? In its present form the text says nothing about child sacrifice in ancient Israel.

If we try to imagine what must have been the mental attitude of Abraham himself (and the narrative is notably silent about this, in contrast to the portrayal of the psychology of the disobedience of Adam and Eve) we are faced squarely with the question of what could have led Abraham to believe that God was asking him to sacrifice another human being. But this is not the only possible starting-point. From Abraham's point of view, the fact that Isaac would live was not known; but for readers, both ancient and modern, the case is different. We *know* the

32

outcome of the story before we read it; we know that God does not really want the life of Isaac, but rather wishes to test Abraham's obedience, and this fact makes all the difference to the way we view the divine command to Abraham. Further, Isaac is not just anybody, and any child would have sufficed if the story were merely about the ending of child sacrifice. Isaac is the means whereby the divine promises to Abraham will be fulfilled, and God's plan for mankind will be accomplished. Thus what is amazing about God's command to Abraham is not that Abraham is directed to kill a child, but that God commands something which threatens to destroy the divine plan for the blessing of mankind through Abraham's descendants. In this way, the narrative expresses God's absolute sovereignty and freedom. If he chooses, he can appear to destroy plans which he seems to have made.

If we are to try to understand the passage in psychological or experiential terms, then we must not try to imagine what Abraham might have thought God was commanding him to do; we must look to the experience of the writer, and of Israel. The Israelites had come to know God as someone good, but unsafe. God could seem far off, he could act as though to destroy his people and annul his promises, yet always his plan was later made clear. The story of the offering of Isaac expresses the fact that the man of faith and the divine community will pass through periods when God's plan seems to be in danger of failure. After the story had been written in its present form, Israel experienced the traumas of the destruction of Jerusalem and the exile to Babylon, and Jeremiah accused God of having deceived him (Jeremiah 20:7). And yet God's purposes had not been frustrated or brought to nothing, and those who continued in obedience in times of great uncertainty often—but not always—saw the answer to their uncertainty.

The modern reader is most unlikely to come to feel that God is commanding him to destroy part of the Christian scheme of salvation. He may, however, be asked to do things that disturb his secue pattern of church life. These may involve giving up familiar buildings and forms of worship, or demand close co-operation with those whose doctrine he distrusts. He may then feel that his view of the divine plan is under attack, and although he should not be passive and uncritical, he should also ponder Genesis 22. The quality of obedience and courage symbolized in the story of Abraham and Isaac will be needed at some time by all those who follow the God of Abraham.

5

JACOB AT JABBOK

Genesis 32: 22–32

It is fascinating to live in an old house, which has been altered from time to time over the years. You may be able to discover that the present dining room was formerly the kitchen, and that the present kitchen was built on to the house some time later, and that there was once a toilet in the basement. Interesting as it is to try to reconstruct the past history of the house, it is the present house in which you have to live.

Genesis 32: 22–32 has been likened to an old house which was added to and altered over the years. Among parts of the basic material can be discerned:

(a) a pun on the name of the river 'Jabbok' (verse 22) (Hebrew *yabbok*) and the verb 'wrestled' (verse 24) (Hebrew *yēābēk*)—evidently, according to one story, the river was called Jabbok because of the wrestling

(b) an explanation of why the Israelites do not eat the sinew of the hip (verses 25, 31–32)

(c) an explanation of why the sanctuary at Penuel was so named (verse 30)

(d) an explanation of the name 'Israel' and an account of why Jacob also bore this name (verse 28; see 35: 10 for another bestowal of the name 'Israel' upon Jacob)

(e) the motif of a river spirit trying to prevent a traveller from crossing.

Because, continuing the analogy of the old house, the original features and purposes of parts of a house can only be guessed from its present structure if we do not possess original plans, there are different opinions about the origin of our passage. Some have compared it with the sort of folk-tale in which spirits have to return to their world before daybreak (compare verse 26). Some have suggested a connexion with a limping ritual dance enacted at Penuel. Others have suggested that the narrative records Israel's conquest of the sanctuary at Penuel, and the incorporation of the worship of its god into the religion of Israel. Others, again, have suggested that the original combatants in the story were Jacob and Esau.

In view of the long and complex evolution of the passage to its present form, it is clearly dangerous to try to explain away its strange elements by saying, for example, that it was a dream dreamed by Jacob on the eve of the crisis of his encounter with Esau (chapter 33). Also, the lack of unanimity among scholars about the original form and meaning of the story should make us cautious about adding to the number of suggestions.

The first thing that can be said about the passage is that like Genesis 18 it concerns the *presence* of God, and that like Genesis 18 it expresses the divine presence in a deliberately confusing way. Thus, just as Abraham did not regard the three visitors as themselves divine, so here, Jacob wrestles with a man, but does not seem to realize that he is more than a man until the latter disables Jacob's thigh by supernatural means. Again, the mystery of the divine presence is retained in that the man refuses to tell Jacob his name, although he has declared that Jacob has prevailed in his wrestling with *God* (verse 28).

It is possible to interpret the story:

(*a*) in terms of the character of Jacob. Verse 28 'thy name shall be no more called Jacob' recalls the bad associations of the name 'Jacob', such as 'supplanter' (Genesis 25:26 RV margin), and reminds us of Jacob's treachery towards his brother Esau, and of his astuteness with his father-in-law Laban. Jacob's encounter with God results in a new character as well as a new name.

(*b*) in terms of the experience of encounter with God on the part of the editor(s). It can be argued that it was the unpleasant, self-seeking side of Jacob's personality (Genesis 28:20–22)'which made him persist in his wrestling. The result was that Jacob's energies were brought more fully into line with God's will, but not without cost to Jacob, as seen in the pain in his thigh, and his subsequent disability (verses 25, 31). Also, the result of Jacob's striving was that his knowledge of God became deeper and more personal (verse 30). By so portraying Jacob, the editor has possibly expressed his understanding of experience of God: that the energies that can make the character of a person unattractive can be put to God's service, that this involves pain, but that a deeper relationship with God results.

35

Can these suggestions in the last two paragraphs be legitimately derived from the text? In one sense, they can no more be objectively supported than can the various suggestions about the original form of the story. Also, like these latter suggestions, their plausibility to each reader depends on the reader's presuppositions. Those who regard Genesis as a collection of primitive stories put together by editors whose moral and religious outlook was far inferior to theirs will presumably be reluctant to go as far as does the exposition here. However, if we allow for some sophistication and genuine experience of God on the part of the editor(s), we may accept that an old, much re-shaped story of probably non-Israelite origin has been used to express the Israelite experience of the mystery of encounter with God, its transforming effect, and its cost to the person involved.

6

THE BURNING BUSH

Exodus 3:1–6

Commentators are generally agreed that the incident of the burning bush originally existed in two separate sources, which have been combined here. Thus, for example, in verse 4, the abrupt change of divine name from 'the Lord' to 'God' can be attributed to the fact that one source usually employed the divine name 'the Lord', while the other used the name 'God' (See Introduction, page 17). However, it has also been accepted that even within the source using 'the Lord', there is an apparent confusion between 'the Lord' and the 'angel of the Lord'. Thus in verse 2 it is the angel who appears and causes the bush to burn, whereas in verse 4 it was presumably 'the Lord' who spoke directly to Moses. The combination of two sources is not itself responsible, then, for the sort of apparent confusion between God and his messengers which we have argued to be characteristic of stories about the *presence* of God. This confusion is found in one of the sources, and its function is to emphasize that while the divine presence is a mystery, yet it was this presence that Moses encountered.

When we turn to consider the burning bush itself, the question asked by most readers is 'what happened?' Conservative commentators have regarded the burning bush as something seen by Moses himself. The fact that it was burning has been explained in terms of a sunset, or as resulting from the full bloom of a bush known as 'burning bush', but such natural explanations have been regarded as less important than the fact that God somehow attracted the attention of Moses to a particular spot, and there spoke his word to Moses.

An explanation in terms of natural phenomena has also been favoured by commentators who are not conservative. They have not supposed that Moses himself saw anything (at least one such commentator has even denied the historical existence of Moses), but have pointed to stories about burning bushes told among other peoples. They have argued that such stories rest ultimately on natural happenings that have been understood by primitive expectation to be manifestations of the divine. The story of the burning bush is, on such a view, an Israelite version of a burning bush story, which is used in the tradition in order to express the divine presence. The story arises from the pre-scientific outlook of the ancient Israelites who 'expected supernatural appearances and . . . were accustomed to explain many events and occurrences as manifestations of the divine' (J. P. Hyatt, *Exodus: New Century Bible*, Oliphants, page 72).

A quite different approach looks for the origin of the burning bush not in an actual observation by someone, but in terms of the growth of the tradition, and literary devices. The Hebrew word for bush (*sneh*) is reminiscent of the name Sinai (Hebrew *sinai*). It is thus possible that the author wished to prepare the reader for the later great revelation at Sinai (Exodus 19). He did not mention Sinai *by name* in chapter 3 (Horeb in verse 1 is regarded by some editors as a later gloss), but *alluded to it* in the word for bush. The flame is also an allusion to the fire in which God descended on to Sinai in 19:18. The connexion between 'bush' and 'Sinai' may have arisen in the oral tradition, but in the present narrative, the burning bush is a deliberate literary allusion to chapter 19. A variation on the same sort of approach would be simply to regard the bush as originating from the pun in Hebrew on 'bush' and 'Sinai'. The *burning* of the bush would originate from the association of angels of God with fire. Thus the Seraphim of Isaiah 6 may be fiery beings (Hebrew *sāraph* = to burn); the cherubim who guarded the tree of life had flaming swords (Genesis 3:24); the angel of God in Judges 6:21 caused an offering to be devoured by fire. It is clear from Exodus 3:2 that the fire is caused by an angel.

These differing explanations are once more only possible because objectives principles for discovering 'what really happened' are lacking. This makes it difficult to give sound guidance. I am inclined to

37

rule out the approach that says that Moses himself saw something, because the narrative is based on third-hand and not a first-person tradition (see Introduction, page 15). The whole story is a kind of shorthand, and the exact 'mechanics' of Moses's call cannot be known. We can only state that our passage is typical of other accounts of the *presence* of God, and, like them, asserts the Israelite conviction that the mystery of the divine presence could be truly known in the world of human experience.

We must turn, then, from the question of 'what happened' to the question 'what does the story mean to convey?' Whatever the exact historical nature of the encounter which is here recorded, as portrayed in the Old Testament it takes place in the course of a man's ordinary routine life. A familiar object is suddenly seen in a new way; there is an awareness of the beauty and awesomeness of holiness, and a human life is entrusted with immense tasks which will bring heartache and failure. Similar themes can be found elsewhere in the Old Testament. Amos tells us (though he does not tell us how) that 'the Lord took me from following the flock, and the Lord said to me, "Go, prophesy to my people Israel"' (Amos 7:15). Isaiah whilst worshipping in the temple, was made aware of the awesomeness of God and was entrusted with a divine task (Isaiah 6). Presumably, worship for Isaiah, and herding the flock for Amos, were routine things, one day to be shot through with new significance. Similarly, our Exodus narrative at least seeks to express that wider experience of ancient Israel of a God who somehow breaks through into the ordinary things of this world, with the purpose of offering deliverance and judgement, through the commitment of those who will follow his call.

7

THE PLAGUES IN EGYPT

Exodus 7:14–10:29, 12:29–36

Here, for the first time, we meet a narrative that is concerned with the *power* of God. In the standard commentaries the plagues receive full treatment, and only general comments are needed here. Readers will find the commentaries by S. R. Driver (Cambridge Bible) and J. P.

Hyatt (New Century Bible) particularly helpful in their general approach to the plagues.

Although there are ten plagues, it has long been recognized that the present narrative is a combination of probably two originally independent sources, which largely, but not completely, overlapped. Thus the plague of boils stands only in the Priestly source, while the plague of flies and cattle-plague are found only in the Yahwistic source. Neither of these originally separate sources probably contained more than eight plagues. The plagues are also referred to in Psalm 78:44—51 and Psalm 105:28—36, where again there are slight differences in the order and nature of the plagues, and where not more than eight plagues are enumerated in either Psalm.

Our present narrative has a certain climactic structure. The requests of Moses to Pharaoh become more demanding, beginning with a request that the Israelites should make a three-day journey into the wilderness to offer sacrifice to God (5:3), and ending in the demand that the whole people, taking their possessions with them, should be allowed to go and serve God in the wilderness (10:24—26). The present narrative, then, has a literary and dramatic structure, although its various sources can be reasonably well discerned.

Interest has understandably centred on the plagues, and their explanation. Conservative commentators, many of whom deny that different sources underlie the narrative, often accept that the plagues were natural occurrences, and see the miracle as resting in the timing of the plagues. A series of natural disasters in Egypt coinciding with the escape of the Israelite slaves is seen as the hand of God in the Exodus process. That the basis in fact of the traditions of the plagues was a natural disaster or disasters is also recognized by most commentators who are not conservative in approach, but they would allow a long and complex process in the growth of the tradition to its present form.

In an appendix to his commentary, Hyatt sets out two attempts to account for the plagues in natural terms. One assumes that they occurred in a year when the level of the Nile was unusually low, and the other assumes the opposite, that the Nile was unusually high. Both explanations try to account for all the plagues recorded in Egypt happening in a comparatively short space of time. Hyatt is right, in my view, to be cautious about such explanations, which make no allowance for the variation in the number and nature of the plagues in the underlying sources or the Psalms traditions. On the basis of this latter evidence, indeed, it must be asserted that although there were undoubtedly some natural disasters in Egypt when a group of Israelite slaves escaped, the exact number and nature of the disasters can never be known. In the course of time, the number of natural disasters has probably been added to as the stories have been told and re-told.

In the complex process that lies between the original events and the narrative in Exodus, folk-tale elements have had their influence, and have left their mark. In folk-tales, a common way in which magic works is by transforming one substance into something else (in Cinderella a pumpkin becomes a coach). Transformations occur in the plagues stories. Thus, the river is transformed into blood, dust is transformed into lice and ashes are transformed into boils. The fact that in folk-tales the forces of magic work on the side of the hero or heroes helps us to understand how the stories of the plagues were influenced and shaped by the folk-tale tradition of the ancient Hebrews. Stories about the natural disasters at the time of the Exodus, advantageous to the Hebrews, matched easily with traditional folk-stories about magic forces assisting the hero. In the course of oral transmission, the plague stories received some of their folk-tale features, for example, the idea that some plagues were produced by a magic rod, and that others were transformations of one substance into another. They also probably received some of the dialogue that now accompanies them, and something of the dramatic form whereby as soon as one plague had ceased, without any effect on Pharaoh's attitude, the next plague was brought about.

To put the implications of the preceding paragraph bluntly, what is being said is that though the traditions of the plagues have a *basis* in fact, and their occurrence at the time of the Exodus can be regarded as miraculous, it is highly unlikely that the interviews between Pharaoh and Moses took place with the dialogue recorded in Exodus. It is highly unlikely that Moses or Aaron waved a rod, or their hand, in order to bring about the plagues. Although we can only guess at what really happened, the likelihood is that the Israelites made an escape from Egypt that was contrary to Egyptian desires at a time of upheaval and confusion accompanied by several natural disasters. We owe it to the development of the stories in the folk tradition that the highly confused situation at the time of the Exodus was interpreted and presented in terms of divine initiative in favour of the Hebrews, that the confusion of events was reduced to an ordered succession of plagues and interviews with Pharaoh, and that this dramatic structure was able to explore the character and obstinacy of Pharaoh.

So far, then, it has been suggested that the oral shaping of recollections about natural disasters at the time of the Exodus was responsible for the magical elements in the narratives in their final forms, and that such oral shaping made possible the theological dimensions which the stories now possess. We must also observe another, and different, process at work. It is generally acknowledged that in the Priestly version of the plagues, the miraculous or supernatural element is heightened in comparison with other sources. For example, this source sometimes adds that a particular plague was also achieved by the Egyptian magicians, although the latter were unable to stop the plague. In the first plague, the Priestly version (see the commentaries for this) describes how all water throughout Egypt turned into blood, whereas the Yahwistic source restricts the miracle to the waters of the Nile. The Priestly source, although containing early traditions, is agreed to have reached its final form latest of all sources, and its heightening of the miraculous is an example of the way in which the further one gets from happenings in point of time, the easier it is to heighten the supernatural. The Priestly account also no doubt wishes to emphasize the transcendence of God.

In conclusion, the moral question has to be raised whether we believe that God would have treated Pharaoh and the Egyptians in the way described in the narratives. In the case of the hardening of Pharaoh's heart, the narrative displays some subtlety, and in its final form there is an apparent contradiction between Pharaoh hardening his own heart (8:32) and God hardening Pharaoh's heart (9:12). The whole theme probably originated in the folklore stage when the dramatic need to present the plagues in a culminating series also required a reason, which was provided by Pharaoh's obstinacy. The final narrative, however, seeks to express both God's complete control over the destinies of men (that is, God hardened Pharaoh's heart), and the part that can be played by a man in shaping his own destiny and those of others (that is, Pharaoh hardened his own heart).

The other moral question is whether God would have smitten the Egyptians with plagues; or to put it another way, what did the Israelites think when they read that God had smitten their foes? I doubt whether we have here an example of Israel's debased moral and spiritual understanding compared with our own supposed higher modern insights. The sort of story in which the 'goody' finally defeats the 'baddy' has long been popular, and in any case is part of folk literature. In our modern society, this story is embodied in 'Westerns' and detective novels. When we, or our young children, thrill to see the 'baddies' being shot down by the 'goodies' on the television screen, we rejoice that good has triumphed, and do not reflect on the disgusting spectacle of murder and killing. The story has become for us a symbol of the triumph of good over evil, and we would not have the story end in any other way.

It is possible that the stories of the plagues had a similar function as they were told, and re-told, in ancient Israel. In times when Israel was in alliance with Egypt, or depended on her for help, the stories would not express God's hatred of Egyptians, but would rather symbolize the victory of God over whatever opposed his purposes. They came to express a belief in the victory of good over evil, on the part of a God whose nature it was to succour the needy and oppressed. But above all, the plagues were part of that wider happening which we call the Exodus, a pattern of events which had far-reaching implications for ancient Israel's consciousness as the people of God, and of her faith in God's power to fulfil his ancient promises. The stories therefore were not only symbolic of the victory of good over evil, but a constant reminder to Israel of God's call to serve him in the fight against evil.

8

THE PILLAR OF CLOUD AND FIRE

Exodus 13:21–22, 14:19, 24, 40:38
Numbers 9:15–23, 10:34, 14:14

The pillar of cloud by day and of fire by night is a symbol for the *presence* of God during the wilderness wanderings. In the Yahwistic source it is a symbol not of an active presence, but of how *God himself* led the Israelites through the wilderness when there was no other leader who knew the way. In the Priestly source, the divine presence seems less active (see especially Numbers 9:15–23). Here, the pillar of cloud covers the tabernacle by day, and the pillar of fire covers it by night when the Israelites are not journeying. The taking-up of the pillar from the tabernacle is a sign that the Israelites are to journey further (Numbers 9:22); its presence is a sign that the camp must remain where it is.

Only the most literalist view of the Bible can accept the narrative at its face value: that an unbroken pillar of cloud travelled at the head of the Israelite caravan, turning at night into a fire. Thus even conservative commentators have allowed themselves a certain freedom in the interpretation of the passage. For example, it has been suggested that a whirlwind sighted in or near the camp was used by God to assure the people of his presence. But even an interpretation that assumes that the pillar of cloud goes back to a whirlwind actually observed by the Israelites in the camp, has to allow that it is not the same as saying that a pillar of cloud actually guided the Israelites through the wilderness. Even on such a conservative view, then, the present narrative is more symbolically and theologically true than literally and historically accurate.

Many commentators have sought the origin of the pillar of cloud and fire in the custom of guiding caravans at night by a lighted brazier or lighted torches. However, it has been rightly objected to this suggestion that it does not explain the origin of the pillar of cloud by day. Neither does it account for the fact that where natural phenomena are the basis for belief in divine manifestations, these are natural phenomena that are unusual and awesome (such as volcanoes), and not in any case of human manufacture. Such a commonplace thing as a man-made torch or brazier is hardly likely to have given rise to a tradition such as that which is our concern here.

A rival theory to the torch or brazier theory is the volcano theory. One writer has cited the 1905 eruption of Vesuvius as a parallel. Apparently the eruption was preceded by the emission of a great cloud of smoke which was visible many miles away, and which seemed to become a pillar of fire at night as the red-hot interior of the volcano shone upwards. Such a phenomenon is more likely to give rise to something like our passage; but the objection to this theory can be raised that there was no volcanic activity in the area of the wilderness wanderings. However, the theory could still stand if it were assumed that volcanic activity, not necessarily anywhere near the wilderness of Sinai nor at the time of the wanderings, had provided a symbol for the divine presence in the folk literature of the ancient Hebrews and surrounding peoples, and that this symbol had been employed in the tradition to describe God's presence among his people in the wilderness. On this view, the important fact would be the Israelite conviction that God's presence had guided his people. The pillar of cloud and fire would be a *means* of expressing this fact. Yet another possibility that has been suggested is that the incense which ascended together with the smoke of offerings from sanctuaries, is the origin of the symbol.

It will be clear once more that a straightforward 'explaining away' of the supernatural will not do justice to the complexities of this tradition,

43

and that ultimately, only a sympathetic theological approach will appreciate its real point. It expresses ancient Israel's conviction not merely of the presence of God, but of his active guiding and leadership through a difficult journey. It is no wonder that the wilderness has been likened to the earthly pilgrimage of religious people, a journey in which God's active presence and guidance have been experienced.

9

THE CROSSING OF THE RED SEA

Exodus 14:15–31

Two basic sources underlying this narrative can be discerned, the one emphasizing the supernatural more than the other. In the Priestly account, verses 15–19, 21a, 21d–23, 26, 28–29, the miracle of the parting of the sea is attributed directly to God. The Israelites walk on dry ground through the sea, which stands like a wall on either side of the path. The Yahwistic version attributes the parting of the sea to 'a strong east wind all the night' (verse 21b) after which the sea returned to its 'wonted flow' (verse 27 RV). However, the Yahwistic version does not lack a supernatural element. In verses 24–25, God causes havoc among the Egyptians; verse 25 may suggest simply that the chariot wheels of the Egyptians were clogged in the sand of the sea bed, but taken together with verse 24, verse 25 implies that in some direct, though unspecified way, God fought against the Egyptians. It is possible that verse 24 has been shaped by the common Old Testament theme that in Israel's battles against her foes, the part played by her armies was small while the part played by God was great (compare Judges 7).

It is to the Yahwistic account that interpreters have looked in their attempts to find a natural underlying cause of the miracle. The two explanations that have most readily suggested themselves have been tidal ebb and flow (on the basis of verse 27) and a hot dry wind (verse 21b), or a combination of both. Explanations in terms of volcanic activity have not commended themselves to more recent commentators. An insoluble aspect of the problem has been the lack of agreement among scholars (a lack of agreement occasioned by lack of firm evidence) as to the site of the deliverance; it is not possible to ascertain which natural explanations would be plausible in relation to the place of the happening.

But is it right to base an explanation in natural terms on the Yahwistic narrative? If, as in the escape from Egypt at the time of the plagues, the whole incident was one of chaos and confusion, who was there with time to observe the natural science aspects of the parting of the waters? Another possibility, then, is that the Yahwistic account is an attempted *Israelite natural explanation* of the miracle. Alternatively, if Exodus 15 is earlier than the Yahwistic account, this ancient poem may have given rise to the Yahwistic and Priestly versions of the crossing of the sea.

Exodus 15:8 reads

'At the blast of thy nostrils the waters piled up,
The floods stood up in a heap . . .'

It can be argued, but not of course proved, that the Yahwist took his east wind from the phrase 'the blast of thy nostrils' and that the Priestly writer based his account on the phrase 'the waters were piled up'. If this latter suggestion is true, it provides us with an example of a different sort of origin for a supernatural story, the case in which elements of an ancient poem are turned literally into a prose account of a miracle. A similar example would be that of the sun standing still during the battle near Gibeon (Joshua 10:12–13). Although it has been powerfully argued that the incident in Joshua rests on an eclipse, it seems more likely that an ancient poem in which Joshua called on the sun not to go down until he had achieved victory, was later made the basis of a prose account which took the poem literally.

Ultimately, it is impossible to achieve any certainty in a discussion of 'what really happened' at the crossing of the sea, though few scholars today doubt that somehow some Israelites escaped and some Egyptians perished at the sea.

Compared with our uncertainty of how exactly the deliverance happened, there is no doubt that the Israelites regarded the Red Sea escape as one of the greatest formative moments in their history. It convinced them that their God was the lord of nature, and they had a lively sense that his deliverance was an expression of his response to Israel's need, and nothing deserved on their part. This is why in both the Priestly and Yahwistic narratives, God's part in the deliverance is all-important, and Israel's part is negligible, if indeed Israel has any part to play.

In one sense, the *lasting influence* that the Red Sea deliverance has had in the life of Israel, ancient and modern is as remarkable as the deliverance itself. Although the deliverance does not differ in kind from many other Old Testament miracles (it is possible to explain it in terms of natural phenomena, so that the miraculous is the coincidence of the natural phenomena with Israel's attempt to escape) it is perhaps the miracle which is to be connected more closely than any other with the phenomenon of Israel as a people believing in its divine election and destiny. It resembles the resurrection in that it challenges us not only to think about the initial formative event, but also to account for the lasting influence of that event in the existence of a community which has so deeply affected the world at large.

10

THE BRAZEN SERPENT

Numbers 21:4–9

The episode of the brazen serpent is one in which the concern to discover the origin of the story has sometimes obscured the theological purpose of the narrative in its present form. As it stands, the story is a good sermon. The Israelites murmur against the deliverance from slavery which God has achieved for them, and in spite of his miraculous provision of water and bread (Exodus 16–17) argue that they lack these things and in any case have no taste for the manna. Their ungratefulness, and disregard for the things that God has provided, leads them into disaster. They are punished by a plague of deadly serpents, and quickly conclude that even the God whom they criticize must be approached if they are to get what they want—freedom from the threat of death through snake bite. Although it was not explicitly stated that the repentance of the people was insincere, this may be inferred from the fact that although God provided a way out for the people, the way out did not operate automatically and to the exclusion of any response on the part of an individual. In fact, the onus was on each person to look in trust at the symbol of God's healing which Moses erected.

The brazen serpent is mentioned in II Kings 18:4, where it is stated that during Hezekiah's reform, the king broke the object in pieces because people had burned incense to it. This passage connects the serpent with Moses. The most popular form of explanation of the incident in Numbers 21 has been that the story is an aetiology (explanatory story) justifying the worship of a serpent in, or in the neighbourhood of,

Jerusalem, by connecting it with Moses. Some have argued that the serpent cult was part of the pre-Israelite religion of Jerusalem, and that the Numbers 21 tradition was generated in order to legitimize the cult as part of Israel's faith. It must be emphasized that if this theory is correct, it tells us only about the *origin* of the story underlying Numbers 21 : 4–9, and does not account for the theological teaching of the narrative in its present form.

Other explanations have been more complex: perhaps the snakes were not actual snakes; the narrative varies between serpents (verse 7) and fiery serpents (verses 6, 8) and the latter may have been demonic beings which were to be warded off by the image which was set up in the camp. Another view is that the setting up of the image was an instance of imitative magic, designed to cure the Israelites from an actual plague of poisonous snakes. Others, again, have linked the story with the snake as a symbol of healing, as sometimes found in connexion with the god Asclepios.

It is more likely that the basis of the story lies in some incident in the wilderness, than in an aetiology legitimizing a pre-Israelite cult practice in Jerusalem. The trouble with labelling something an aetiology is that so many unanswerable questions are raised. Why was the object legitimized by being connected with Moses in particular? Why did the aetiology take the story form that it did? Better knowledge of how aetiologies work has led recent writers on the subject to argue that it is most usual for an *existing* story to be linked to an *existing* practice or fact, and to be seen as the explanation of the latter. It is rarer for a story in all its details to be 'generated' in order to explain what often only corresponds to *one* detail in the story. The association of the brazen serpent with Moses in II Kings 18 : 4 is likely to be correct historically, and this may be supported by the recent discoveries at Timnah. Here, copper workings have been discovered, as well as a Midianite tent shrine in which was a copper serpent. The connexion of Moses with Midian is well attested in the tradition (Exodus 18).

It goes without saying that as it stands, the story displays deep insight into the nature of human attitudes to God. It describes the ever-present drive in human nature which wishes to convert the things of God into personal advantage; it shows how quickly disregard for God can be replaced by requests for his help, either where all else has failed or where human contentment has been disrupted. In meeting such situations, the divine response is not to meet human need in exactly the way people want, but to meet it so that faith and trust in God are renewed and strengthened. This, I believe, is the meaning of the story as it now stands, whatever the stages by which it reached its present form.

In the Apocrypha, Wisdom 16:5 ff. takes up the passage, emphasizing that the purpose of the plague was to draw the people back to God, and that it was not the brazen serpent itself that healed, but God and his word (Wisdom 16:7, 12). In John 3 :14, we may perhaps be entitled to interpret the allusion to Numbers 21:4–9 as follows: Nicodemus seems to have difficulty in believing that Jesus is a teacher sent from God. Although Jesus tries to help the enquirer to overcome his difficulties (John 3:8) he refers finally to our passage in order to emphasize that ultimately, there is no automatic divine deliverance, and that there is an onus on the individual to trust in God's promises.

11

GIDEON'S FLEECE

Judges 6:36–40

The story of Gideon contains a typical example of a tradition about the *presence* of God (Judges 6:11–24). All the features of similar traditions which already have been discussed (see page 14) are present. There is an apparent confusion between the angel of God and God himself; Gideon does not immediately recognize the angel as a supernatural being; the angel is associated with fire; Gideon finally realizes that he has seen an angel of God and expects to die. The comments on other similar passages, and in the Introduction, should help the reader here.

In contrast, the incident of Gideon's fleece is about the *power* of God. It is in no way deeply embedded in its context; it also interrupts the flow of the narrative from 6:35 to 7:1. It shows close affinities with popular folk-belief. The hero seeks a sign, and prays that a fleece left out over-night should be wet with dew, while the ground is dry. When this wish is granted, Gideon seeks further confirmation by asking for the fleece to remain dry, but for the ground to be wet. It goes against too much that is said elsewhere in the Old Testament about signs and trust in God that we should take the narrative at its face value. The story shows all the signs of being a piece of folklore which has entered into the Old Testament without being properly assimilated to the deeper theological insights often displayed by the editors. The request for a sign to be repeated with the conditions the opposite of what has just happened, can be paralleled from non-Israelite folk-belief and practice. Only in respect of the diffidence shown by Gideon in his dealings with God does the story contain anything of permanent value.

12

THE CALL OF SAMUEL

I Samuel 3 : 1–18

The story of the call of Samuel is a variation on traditions about the *presence* of God. In this case, there is no apparent confusion between God and his angel, perhaps because the incident is set inside the temple at Shiloh (verse 3). However, we do find the theme that the divine is not immediately recognized for what it is. Three times, Samuel mistakes the voice of God for that of Eli.

The question that some readers wish to ask is whether this was an audial experience on the part of Samuel, that is, whether he actually heard a voice calling and speaking to him. The narrative assumes that he did, and as I have said in the Introduction (page 15) we must allow that some people genuinely claim to have had such experiences. However, it is also possible that because this is an account based on the third-hand tradition of encounter between God and man, there has been a heightening of the directness of the communication in the story, and that if we had had a narrative stemming from a first-hand tradition of what Samuel experienced, the story would have taken a more indirect form.

There are also indications in the narrative that it has been shaped and rounded off by oral transmission or by deliberate literary device. The threefold repetition of an incident (verses 4–8) is typical of folk-tales, and serves to heighten the climax of the story, which is the message which Samuel receives from God. Samuel's response to God's calling:

'speak; for thy servant heareth'

has often been used as a prayer by those seeking God's will, and the fact that it was, in the narrative, a response taught by Eli to Samuel (verse 9) may suggest that it formed part of religious instruction from priests or parents to their children. Such instruction would reflect the Old Testament conviction, expressed powerfully in the whole incident, that God 'speaks' to his people, for consolation and for judgement.

49

13

THE PLAGUES BROUGHT UPON THE PHILISTINES BY THE ARK

I Samuel 5:1–7:1

It can be regarded as certain that at some stage during the late 11th century BC, the ark of the covenant was captured by the Philistines from the Israelites, and then later returned. The stories of I Samuel 5:1–7:1 give an explanation *why* the ark was returned. They tell of the *power* of the ark as a holy object, and thus indirectly of the power of God. Most commentators look for the origin of the traditions about why the ark was returned in popular stories about the ark and its power.

According to the tradition, the ark affected the Philistines in two or three ways. First, the image of the god Dagon fell down in his temple in Ashdod, and then was mutilated. Second, the people of Ashdod, and subsequently of other places to which the ark was sent, were smitten with some sort of ailment such as boils and haemorrhoids. Possibly, third, they were plagued with rats (cp. 5:6 RV margin and NEB text). In the account of the misfortunes of the statue of Dagon, the incident explains a custom observed by priests and worshippers at the temple of Dagon.

It is quite feasible that the reason why the Philistines returned the ark was that its capture coincided with an outbreak of plague possibly caused by rats. The golden symbols of the plagues (6:4, 18) which were returned with the ark would in this case be charm objects to ward off the afflictions. It is more difficult to comment on the misfortunes of Dagon's image. If the information of 5:5 that visitors to the temple avoided treading on the threshold is correct, and if this fact was known to the Israelites, the story of the mutilation of the idol could have arisen in order to explain the custom.

The whole narrative in its present form shows signs of theological editing. The plagues which afflicted the Philistines are likened to the plagues in Egypt (6:6), and a contrast is drawn between the Egyptians who did not respond to the power of God displayed in the plagues, and the Philistines who were prudent enough to return the ark. Although the aim of the narrative is to display the superior power of the God of Israel over other gods, the whole incident contains a warning for the people of God. The ark was lost in the first place because the Israelites believed that it guaranteed victory whatever their moral attitude might be

(I Samuel 4). In this, they were profoundly mistaken. The purpose of the stories of the Philistine misfortunes after their capture of the ark is to show that the God of Israel is still the victor in spite of his people's defeat. Indeed, the incident reinforces the point that the loss of the ark was God's will, and part of his plan to teach his people first, that their moral attitudes were important (compare I Samuel 2:12–3:21) and second, that God would sweep away any symbol of his presence that became a substitute for his presence, and that was manipulated for human gain. In this last sense, the whole incident looks forward to the loss of the Jerusalem temple in 587 BC and to the bitterness of exile in which Israel was forced, through suffering, to learn deeper lessons about the divine plan.

14

ELIJAH'S DROUGHT

I Kings 17–18

The traditions about Elijah and Elisha present some features not previously encountered. Although the stories are third-hand traditions, the directness of divine communication that usually characterizes such stories is absent. Whereas elsewhere we have 'The Lord said unto Moses' or 'The Lord said to Samuel', in the Elijah and Elisha cycles the matter is more indirect. The word of the Lord comes to Elijah (for example 17:2, 8), although we are not told how. The great revelation of God on Mount Horeb (I Kings 19) has a sense of transcendence and immanence, as well as mystery. Elisha on one occasion depends on a music-induced trance to receive a message from God (II Kings 3:15). Whatever may be the reason for this fundamental difference, Elijah and Elisha certainly mark a transition between the tradition about the great men of God of Israel's period before there was a king, and the tradition stemming from the prophets of the 8th century onwards. Elijah and Elisha were active at the time when historical records were being kept, and were involved in national and international politics. Whereas only the vaguest details about the life and character of Moses are known for certain, it is possible to build up a fuller picture of Elijah. At the same time, the figures of Elijah and Elisha have attracted to themselves the sort of miraculous tales that centre on the exploits of mysterious holy men. Thus, on the one hand, we are dealing, in Elijah, with a clear historical character, while on the other hand, aspects of his work have been undoubtedly embellished by folk tradition.

In discussing Elijah's drought, we are faced with this problem: if we accept the account as substantially true, then why not do the same for the nature miracles of Moses? This is a fair question. If we accept on the grounds of faith and philosophical theology that God is active in the world in response to the prayers of his servants, and that Elijah was one of a select group of people whose outsized demands and burning conviction had amazing results, then why not add Moses to that select group, and treat his demands for miracles in exactly the same way? In one sense, it cannot be denied that the plagues in Egypt can be treated in exactly the same way as Elijah's drought. Both sets of phenomena were meant to bring a hostile king to his senses. But if interpreters have not treated Moses and Elijah alike, the reason lies in the *nature* of the traditions about the two men. As has been pointed out (see page 40) the traditions about the plagues show signs of folk-tale influences both in form and content, and this leads me to regard them as *later reflections*, on historical happenings which cannot be clearly determined. The tradition of Elijah's drought, although some folk-tales have been *attached to it* (compare I Kings 17:8–24), shows no signs of influence by folk tradition, and it would have been hard for such a story to gain credence if a drought of severe proportions had not affected a large number of people, and been remembered for some time after.

It is difficult to say whether Elijah prayed that there should be no rain, or whether he interpreted a drought as being God's punishment. Possibly both suggestions have some truth. If we take the contest on Mount Carmel and the ending of the drought (I Kings 18:43–46) as part of the drought story, Elijah displays a combination of shrewd observation, and unwavering faith in God's response to the requests of his servants. It has often been pointed out that the best natural explanation of the fire from heaven is lightning, and that such lightning could precede the heavy rains that quickly followed the contest on Mount Carmel. I Kings 18:1 indicates a link between the reappearance of Elijah after his hiding away from Ahab, and the coming of rain. A good knowledge of climatic conditions could have been, on the human side, the signal for Elijah to return and to set up the contest on Mount Carmel. On the other hand, it would be in keeping with the character of Elijah that he make no great distinction between what experience had taught him, and what he felt God was leading him to do. The whole point of the contest on Mount Carmel was that it was to be an authentication of the power of the God of Israel, and this was only achieved in all honesty by a man of the deepest faith putting that faith at risk. There may have been thunder in the air, but the miracle was that the lightning struck where Elijah prayed that the fire of God would descend.

At the end of the drought story we have Elijah running perhaps some twenty miles, and reaching Jezreel before Ahab's chariot did. It is possible that Elijah achieved this remarkable feat. We have to remember that he was an ascetic man living a largely outdoor life, and he could well have possessed unusual physical powers. Such a fact would fit in well with his fiery devotion to God, as well as with the fact that folk-tales were later attracted to the traditions about him.

15

VARIOUS MIRACLES OF ELIJAH AND ELISHA

Elijah fed by ravens	(I Kings 17 : 3—7)
The barrel of meal and the cruse of oil	(I Kings 17 : 14—16)
Elijah restores a dead boy	(I Kings 17 : 17—24)
Elijah brings fire down from heaven on his would-be captors	(II Kings 1 : 9—16)
Elijah's mantle	(II Kings 2 : 8, 14)
Elisha purifies water	(II Kings 2 : 19—22)
Boys who revile Elisha are killed by bears	(II Kings 2 : 23—24)
The pot of oil	(II Kings 4 : 1—7)
Elisha restores the Shunammite's son	(II Kings 4 : 18—37)
Elisha's staff	(II Kings 4 : 29—31)
Elisha purifies poisoned food	(II Kings 4 : 38—41)
Elisha multiplies food	(II Kings 4 : 42—44)
Gehazi is struck with leprosy	(II Kings 5 : 20—27)
Elisha makes the axehead swim	(II Kings 6 : 1—7)
Elisha's bones restore a dead man	(II Kings 13 : 20—21)

It is convenient to take together some of the miracles recorded in the Elijah/Elisha cycles. An examination of their number and nature indicates that they constitute a unique block of material in the Old Testament. It is true that a number of miracles are recorded in the accounts of the wilderness wanderings, including the incidents of the manna, the quails and the provision of water from the rock; but these latter miracles can easily be explained in terms of the natural resources in the Sinai desert, and in any case, they have been so deeply assimilated into the distinctive theology of the Old Testament that their primary function is to teach lessons about obedience and faithfulness to God. What is unique about the Elijah/Elisha miracles is their quantity, and the fact that in many cases they have not been assimilated to the theological purposes of their wider context.

Some of the stories point clearly to folk-tale as their immediate source. The miracle of the pot of oil is a typical example of the way in which in folk-tales magic forces assist those in need. Although there is no doubt that Elijah sought refuge with a poor widow of Zarephath, the account of the miracle worked on her behalf to give her and her son food, is clearly a folk-tale. Elijah's destruction by fire of soldiers sent to capture him expresses the dislike in folk-tales of hostile royal officers, whilst the transference of Naaman's leprosy to Gehazi is a popular way of describing the punishment of a trickster. Because of the folklore origin of the stories, it is not surprising to find duplicate stories. Thus six of them have to do with the miraculous provision of food or the purifying of contaminated food and water. The six are the miracles of the ravens, the barrel of meal and cruse of oil, the pot of oil, the purifying of water, the purifying of poisoned food, and the multiplication of food. Both prophets restore a dead boy to life, and Elisha's bones resuscitate a dead man. Because of the partial overlap of the miracles attributed to Elijah and Elisha, some historians have argued that only one of them actually existed (there are other difficulties also about the reconstruction of the history of Israel in this period). However, the two figures are too firmly connected with trustworthy historical narratives in the biblical record to sustain such a view, and the reason why their miracles overlap somewhat is that both figures have attracted to themselves typical folk-tale motifs.

Although in many cases, it is now impossible to ascertain what, if anything, is the historical basis underlying the miracles, not all of the stories are to be regarded in the same way. The destruction of forty-two children by two she-bears (II Kings 2:23–24) has a circumstantial ring about it. In its present form, there may be some telescoping, in that the ravaging of children by she-bears may have been understood as a punishment for mocking the man of God sometime earlier; in the biblical version, the telescoping made the bears come out from a wood as soon as Elisha had uttered his curse. However, an historical basis can be credibly reconstructed here. In the stories of purifying water or food,

54

the historical basis may well be that men like Elijah and Elisha had the knowledge of what we today call herbalism. Such a holy man would be consulted by a city whose water supply was polluted.

Several of the incidents have been worked into larger contexts, so as to carry a theological message. The widow of Zarephath (I Kings 17) is a foreigner and not a believer in the God of Israel. Yet her readiness to help the man of God, even to her last food, contrasts with the attitude of persons like King Ahab and his steward Obadiah, the former of whom has rejected his God, and the latter of whom is reluctant to make any sacrifice for his faith (I Kings 18:7 ff.). One is incidentally reminded here of the sort of folk-tale in which a wish quoted by a stranger enables a humble person to be enriched, whereas calculating, well-to-do people are unable to turn the wish to their own advantage. The incident of Elijah bringing fire on his would-be captors was probably already well shaped in the folk tradition. One notes that the incident happened three times. In its present form, however, the incident teaches the inadvisability of insolence to the servants of God, and counsels humility (II Kings 1:3). The purpose of the account of Elijah's mantle is to show that Elisha has truly succeeded to Elijah's office, and that God has not left his people in Israel without a guardian, at a time when faith in the God of Israel is under severe attack.

We can say that taken together, these stories reflect something of the Old Testament belief that while much that happens in the world is reasonable and predictable, God, in his relation to the world causes the unexpected and the mysterious to happen, and thereby warns man against trying to exclude the creator from his creation.

16

THE ASCENSION OF ELIJAH

II Kings 2:1–18

The taking up to heaven of a hero beloved of the gods is a theme found in the ancient Near East outside Israel. Nor is the ascension of Elijah unique in the Old Testament, although it is certainly the only explicit account of such a happening. In Genesis 5:24 it is reported that 'Enoch walked with God: and he was not; for God took him', and some commentators have seen allusions to the 'taking' of a man by God to himself in Psalm 49:15—'But God will ransom my soul from the power of

Sheol: for he will receive me', and in Psalm 73:24—'Thou shalt guide me with thy counsel, And afterward thou wilt receive me to glory'. Possibly too in Psalm 16:10–11—'For thou dost not give me up to Sheol, or let thy godly one see the Pit. Thou dost show me the path of life, in thy presence there is fullness of joy, in thy right hand are pleasures for evermore'.

As it stands, the narrative of Elijah's ascension is compounded of a number of elements. First, it has often been noted that the main character in the story is not Elijah but Elisha, and that the episode amounts to a prophetic 'calling' of Elisha. In this connexion, the narrative makes a point about the need for loyalty and persistence: Elisha will only receive the blessing which he seeks if he stays close to Elijah until the end (verse 10), and he has to resist Elijah's attempts to leave him behind (verses 4, 6). A second theme, which was noticed under section 15 is that of Elijah's mantle and its magical properties; but here, it symbolizes the spirit of Elijah, and marks Elisha as the true successor of his master. Third, there is the phrase, 'My father, my father, the chariots of Israel and its horsemen!' (verse 12). This phrase is found also in II Kings 13:14 when it is said as Elisha's death is perceived to be near. There may also be an allusion to it in II Kings 6:17, where Elisha's servant sees that although he and his master are in danger, they are surrounded by heavenly hosts of horses and chariots. It has been suggested that the phrase expresses a conviction and a prayer: a conviction that so long as Elijah was among the people, the powers of God were available through him to protect the people who were faithful to God against the threats of Jezebel; and a prayer that this protection would not be withdrawn after Elijah's departure.

The general reader wishes to know 'what happened' and how the tradition of Elijah's ascension came into being. The likelihood is that the place and circumstances of Elijah's death were unknown. The tradition about him indicates that he led a roving life, and that while the groups of prophets at certain places (some of them are mentioned in this passage) regarded him as their master, he was often absent from them. It is possible that our passage contains a hint of a search to find his dead body (verse 16–18), although, in its present form, this incident expresses a contrast between the certainty of Elisha and the doubt of the other prophets about the fate of their master.

If the place and circumstances of Elijah's death were unknown, the story of his ascension would have grown up, first, with the help of the fact that the idea of being 'taken up' was not confined to Israel alone, and second, with the help of the phrase about the chariots and horsemen.

The theological importance of the narrative, however, is that it expresses a conviction that fellowship with God is something that cannot, in cases of men like Elijah, be severed by death. It is often said that the Israelites had no belief in life after death, and that all men were doomed to a shadowy existence in Sheol, where God's power and presence were questionable. But belief in the afterworld is often far from logical (many modern church-goers apparently see no logical contradiction in thinking both of a Last Judgement and of immediately entering God's nearer presence when they die), and while the overwhelming belief of ancient Israel was no doubt concerning the hopelessness of afterlife in Sheol, a small but separate strand, represented by the ascension of Elijah and possibly the other passages listed at the beginning of this section, implies otherwise.

Perhaps the point can be better put by saying that Israel's traditional belief was concerned most with the 'where' of the afterlife. Although there is an inescapable spatial element in the idea of being 'taken' to God, the main point is that it speaks of *quality* of relationship. Can fellowship with God such as that established by a man like Elijah be cut short by death? The answer of the Old Testament was 'no', although in giving this answer it did not work out any new geography of the hereafter. For Christians, indeed, the idea of fellowship with God which cannot be broken by death would perhaps be a better way of speaking than some of their traditional language about the afterlife. In the Old Testament, it is the quality of fellowship with God achieved by a rare soul like Elijah that endures. The New Testament goes further, and speaks of a relation with God which he *bestows* on human beings who are not great saints. According to the New Testament, death cannot separate us from the love of God which is in Christ Jesus (Romans 8:38–39).

17

THE HEALING OF NAAMAN

II Kings 5:1–19

Although the Hebrew word for 'leprosy' includes the disease which modern readers associate with this word, it also denoted in biblical times lesser skin disorders. (See the article 'Leprosy' in *Hastings Dictionary of the Bible*, 2nd edition in one volume, 1956). Naaman's complaint, which apparently did not bar him from all contact with other persons, was probably of the lesser type. However, the main point of the narrative is to stress the 'ordinariness' of the miracle, and the importance of obedience to those who speak in God's name. Naaman expects Elisha to act in a spectacular way in performing the miracle (verse 11); instead, he is asked to do a simple thing on his own, without his high rank being acknowledged by the prophet. Thus the miracle depends as much on Naaman's obedience and humility, as on Elijah's power. The whole narrative is interesting in comparison with other incidents in the Elijah/Elisha cycle, for it is a counter-balance to the more spectacular miracles. Just as the word which came to Elijah on Mount Carmel was not in the spectacular but in the unspectacular (I Kings 19:11–12), so here, quiet obedience to God's orders is indicated as the way of power.

The conclusion of the story, in which Naaman asks for some earth to take with him to symbolize the presence of God, is not necessarily a sign of primitiveness. Many modern people find it easier to pay respects to their departed loved ones by caring for a grave, than by seeing a name in a book of remembrance at a Crematorium, because the grave focuses their feelings in a way that a name in a book can not. So, similarly, it was asking a lot of a man like Naaman to worship the God of Israel without the help of a tangible symbol. But alongside these seemingly crude approaches to the divine presence, must be put passages such as I Kings 8:27:

> But will God indeed dwell on the earth? behold, heaven and the highest heaven cannot contain thee; how much less this house which I have built!

18

THE VISION OF WATERS FLOWING FROM THE TEMPLE

Ezekiel 47:1–12

Several years ago, Professor Zimmerli of Göttingen completed a commentary on Ezekiel which had taken him 14 years to write, and which was finally 1,285 pages long; yet he has admitted that in spite of all his labours on the book, not to mention the labours of others, there remain many unsolved mysteries in connexion with it. Chapter 47:1–12 shares some of these problems. The Hebrew text has certain awkwardnesses and inconsistencies (see the standard commentaries), and the passage shares with many other parts of the prophecy the problem of how we are to understand the visions. Were they basically real visions experienced by a man of unusual psychical make-up, or are they simply literary devices; or are they a combination of both factors? Commentators are agreed on one point, however, that in spite of its technical difficulties, 47:1–12 contains a clear message.

In our explanations in this book, we have distinguished between narratives based on first- and third-hand tradition. 47:1–12 is probably based on first-hand tradition coming from the prophet himself, although we do not know how directly the prophet was involved in its actual composition and writing. Like other first-hand traditions we have considered, it has the quality of indirectness. The whole action is a vision, and God is represented by a heavenly interpreter.

The vision draws together many biblical symbols, as well as symbols from the geography of Palestine. The waters which trickled out from the Temple (verse 2) recall the words of Psalm 46:4, 'There is a river, whose streams make glad the city of God.'

In fact, no river as such flows anywhere near Jerusalem, and the words of Ezekiel 47:1–12 and Psalm 46 are probably an ancient Israelite expression of the widespread belief in the ancient Near East that from the place where God or the gods dwelt, there flowed a life-giving river or rivers. Genesis 2:10, which describes how a river flowed from the Garden of Eden, is another expression of the same idea. No doubt in ancient times the Jerusalem spring named Gihon was believed to be the visible sign in Jerusalem of the presence of the river of paradise beneath the city.

In opposition to the life-giving waters of the river of God, the passage mentions the deathly waters of the Salt or Dead Sea. These waters, more than 1,000 feet below sea level, and containing a mineral concentration of 24%—26%, support no life, and bring immediate death to any fish brought into them by the River Jordan, which discharges into the Dead Sea. Whatever may be the origin of the story of the destruction of Sodom and Gomorrah (Genesis 19), the story no doubt owes something of its content to the weird and inhospitable landscape which surrounds the Dead Sea, so that the latter may not only symbolize death, but also the depths of human wickedness for which the names Sodom and Gomorrah are Old Testament symbols.

The way in which Ezekiel 47:1–12 describes the healing and life-giving effects of the waters from the temple needs no further explanations and the main message is clear: God's power will turn death into life. Two points must be specially noted, however. The time at which the vision was written down was probably still a time of apparent defeat for Israel. The temple was probably in ruins, and the people of God in exile in Babylon. Yet the certainty of the prophet that God would be victorious was unshakable, and he expressed this conviction in one of the most powerful visions of the Old Testament.

Secondly, it has been noted that what issued from the temple was not the mighty river in which a man could swim, though that is what the waters became (verse 5), but a trickle (verse 2). This puzzle is not explained in the passage; indeed the fact that the whole incident is a vision makes such explanation inappropriate, for we expect odd things to happen in visions. The fact, however, that the waters begin in a trickle is a point of great importance. Like the parables of the seed growing secretly and the mustard seed in the New Testament, our passage warns us that God's ways and beginnings in the world are often small and ordinary, and it needs a visionary to see their ultimate effects and victory.

19

THE BURNING FIERY FURNACE

Daniel 3

The book of Daniel is set, according to its own information, in 6th century Babylon, where the Jews are in exile. However, it has long been believed by commentators that this setting is a literary device, and that in fact the book was written to encourage Jews to remain loyal to their faith in the face of the persecutions of Antiochus IV round about 165 BC. The bulk of the material was probably from the outset symbolic or allegorical in character, and although some of the incidents in the stories may owe something to deeds that kings had done, or sufferings which Jews had suffered, there is no need for us to ask the question 'what really happened?' That question is no more appropriate here than in respect of Ezekiel 47:1–12 (see section 18).

The story of Shadrach, Meshach and Abed-nego is probably an example of the martyr type of story. Because Daniel plays no part in it, it may once have existed independently of the other material in the book, in some form or other. The story contains two main messages: first, that in God's world, however the forces opposed to God may seem to triumph and to defeat God's servants who remain loyal, the truth is that God and his servants are really victorious. The second message is that God's enemies are often reconciled to him through the sufferings of his servants.

In the incident of the burning fiery furnace, the miraculous elements are deliberately heightened so as to express the conviction that God alone is ultimately victorious. The heat of the furnace kills the men whose task it is to throw the prisoners into it (verse 22), and the king sees a fourth man, a divine messenger who symbolizes the presence and power of God, walking with the other three, all of whom are unharmed. Thus Shadrach, Meshach and Abed-nego have a happy outcome to their ordeal. Yet the account is not foolhardy enough to promise that this will be the case for every one of God's servants in similar positions. The three heroes assert (verses 17–18):

> our God whom we serve is able to deliver us from the burning fiery furnace ... But if not, be it known to you, O King, that we will not serve your gods ...

The words 'but if not' recognize that for many, even possibly for all of God's servants, there will be no miraculous deliverance. But taken with the story that follows, the words 'but if not' imply that the God who delivered Shadrach, Meshach and Abed-nego *from* death, will not allow other servants of his to be harmed *by* death.

The same points can be made about the second main message of the passage. In the story (though not in history) Shadrach, Meshach and Abed-nego lived to see Nebuchadnezzar acknowledge the God of Israel as the true God. Many servants of God would not have a similar satisfaction with regard to their persecutors. But the story invites them to trust that their sufferings will not be wasted.

The sceptic will ask whether all this is not really wishful thinking; nobody knows what happens after death, he will say, and incredible stories like that in Daniel 3 prove only that some people will believe any nonsense. However, the writers of Daniel 3 could look back over the history of Israel and see several examples of defeat turned into victory, and of persecutors reconciled to God. Jeremiah stands out as the supreme failure who was victorious (though he did not appreciate his victory), while in Isaiah 52:13 ff., those who have persecuted the Servant of God confess that they had been healed through his sufferings. Thus our story draws upon, and sums up, in a sort of parable, Israel's past experience of God at work. The exaggerations of the miraculous which the story contains serve to express the underlying conviction in the reality of unseen power. The story also looks forward to the New Testament in the way in which it brings together the role of suffering laid upon God's servants and the certainty of victory in what appears to the world to be defeat.

PART III

ACTIVITY SUGGESTIONS

The aim of the following material is to enable readers, singly, or in groups, to test out some of the points explained in the Introduction and the examples. For instance, many people are bothered by the fact that if they decide that one miracle in the Old Testament is based on uncertain historical evidence, this seems to cast doubt on all the miracles. Section I attempts to give readers *objective* criteria for distinguishing, on literary grounds, between types of miracle story, as a preliminary to drawing conclusions about 'what happened'. The other sections deal with differences between narratives about the *power* of God and his *presence*, and with narratives based on first-hand and third-hand tradition.

Each section will need a good deal of time—at least two hours—if it is to be done properly. If the sections are tackled as group activities, it may be possible to apportion the work. For example, in section I, members of the group could divide up the accounts between them, and then having answered the questions separately, collate the results at the end. Others may prefer to discuss each question within the whole group.

I freely admit that I am open to the charge that I have selected the passages and framed the questions in such a way that the results will come out as I wish them! However, I believe the matter is not quite so subjective as that. My aim is that readers should be able to test out for themselves what this book is about, so that they can then apply the principles they learn to other parts of the Old Testament.

It is suggested that the activities are done either with the Revised Version or the Revised Standard Version of the Bible. Groups who used this material at the 'trial' stage, found that the verse numbering in the New English Bible sometimes differed from that in other versions, and that it was not always easy to see in the NEB where verses began and ended.

1

Task:
To examine the Elijah/Elisha miracles in order to see what types of stories are involved.

Material to be studied:

I Kings 17:1–24; 18:17–38, 41–46
II Kings 1:1–16; 2:1–18, 19–22, 23–25; 3:13–20; 4:1–7, 32–36,
38–41, 42–44; 5:1–19; 6:1–7, 8–19; 13:20–21.
(It is appreciated that you have a lot of ground to cover, but the more
you cover, the fuller will be the results).

Method:

1. Make a list of the miracles that you find in these passages.
2. See which of the following descriptions apply to each miracle—
   (a) the story is brief and self-contained. (Put a+ if yes and a— if no,
       and similarly for the other assessments.)
   (b) the spectators are individuals or a small group of people.
   (c) the miracle is inexplicable in natural terms.
   (d) incidents are repeated three or several times.
   (e) the miracle demonstrates the power of the holy man rather than
       the direct power of God.
   (f) the miracle can be paralleled from folk-tales or legends known to
       you.
   (g) the incident expresses no distinctively biblical teaching about
       God.
   (h) put any other characteristic(s) that occur to you as you study the
       passages.

Now set out your results as follows:-

Name of miracle	a	b	c	d	e	f	g	h	
....	+	+			—	—			
....		—	—	+	+				etc.

Can you group the miracles on the basis of these results?

Would you care to make any comments or suggestions about historicity
on the basis of your results?

2

Task:

To study some of the passages about the *presence* of God, and to record
what you think are their common features.

Material to be studied:

Genesis 18:1–19:1; 28:10–17; 32:22–32;
Exodus 3:1–15; 33:17–23; 34:29–35;
I Kings 19:9–13a; Job 38:1–3 and 42:1–2, 5–6;
Ezekiel 1:4–28; Daniel 3:19–25.

Method:

1. Consider how the narratives treat the following points (note—each point will not necessarily apply to each narrative):
   (a) the feelings of the human person(s) involved.
   (b) the reactions of the human person(s) involved.
   (c) what natural phenomena or elements accompany the divine presence?
   (d) how are these natural phenomena or elements used in the story?
   (e) is the presence of God clearly described or
      (i) is God 'confused' with angels or messengers?
      (ii) are qualifying words, such as 'like', 'in the likeness of', 'as it were' used?
   (f) are there any other common features to be found in *at least three* or more of the stories?
2. Describe in your own words what you think is most striking about these passages, taken as a whole.

3

Task:

To examine some narratives based on first-hand tradition of experience of God, or communion with him, in the Old Testament.

Material to be studied:

Nehemiah 2:1–4	Jeremiah 1:11–19; 18:1–11
Psalm 22:1–11	Ezekiel 2:1–3:3
Psalm 51	Hosea 1:1–9
Isaiah 6:1–8	Amos 8:1–2

Method:

Consider the following questions in relation to the passages (not each question will necessarily apply in each case):
   (a) can the divine message be associated with some definite object or event in the person's life, if so, what?

(b) can you suggest a convincing psychological explanation for the human side of the encounter?

(c) detail the human emotions and reactions expressed in the passage.

(d) are any symbols or images used to express the divine presence; if so, what is their possible source?

(e) in what ways does your own experience match the experiences described here?

4

Task:
To examine some narratives based on third-hand tradition of experience of God, or communion with him, in the Old Testament.

Material to be studied:

Genesis 12:1–9	I Samuel 9:15–17
Genesis 26:24–25	I Samuel 14:36–46
Exodus 9:1–7	II Samuel 2:1–4
Exodus 25:1–9	II Kings 19:14–21
Leviticus 19:1–8	

Method:
Consider the following questions in relation to the passages (not each question will necessarily apply in each case):

(a) can the divine message be associated with some definite object or event in the life of the human person involved?

(b) is the encounter with God direct or indirect?

(c) does the passage describe the human emotions or reactions of the participant?

(d) are any symbols or images used to express the divine presence?

(e) does the passage give any indication about how the message might have come from God?

(f) compare your results with those under section 3. Can you make any generalizations, on the basis of the passages studied in both cases, of differences between the first-hand and third-hand accounts?